1st EDITION

Perspectives on Modern World History

Woodstock

1st EDITION

Perspectives on Modern World History

Woodstock

Louise I. Gerdes

Editor

GREENHAVEN PRESS
A part of Gale, Cengage Learning

GALE
CENGAGE Learning·

Detroit • New York • San Francisco • New Haven, Conn • Waterville, Maine • London

Elizabeth Des Chenes, *Managing Editor*

© 2012 Greenhaven Press, a part of Gale, Cengage Learning.

Gale and Greenhaven Press are registered trademarks used herein under license.

For more information, contact:
Greenhaven Press
27500 Drake Rd.
Farmington Hills, MI 48331-3535
Or you can visit our Internet site at gale.cengage.com.

For product information and technology assistance, contact us at
Gale Customer Support, 1-800-877-4253.

For permission to use material from this text or product, submit all requests online at
www.cengage.com/permissions.

Further permissions questions can be e-mailed to permissionrequest@cengage.com.

Articles in Greenhaven Press anthologies are often edited for length to meet page requirements. In addition, original titles of these works are changed to clearly present the main thesis and to explicitly indicate the author's opinion. Every effort is made to ensure that Greenhaven Press accurately reflects the original intent of the authors. Every effort has been made to trace the owners of copyrighted material.

Cover image @ Bettmann/Corbis

LIBRARY OF CONGRESS CATALOGING-IN-PUBLICATION DATA

Woodstock / Louise I. Gerdes, editor.
    p. cm. -- (Perspectives on modern world history)
      Summary: Woodstock: historical background on Woodstock; Controversies surrounding Woodstock; Personal narratives--Provided by publisher.
    Includes bibliographical references and index.
    ISBN 978-0-7377-5798-9 (hardback)
1. Woodstock Festival--History. 2. Popular culture--United States--History--20th century.
3. Counterculture--United States--History--20th century. I. Gerdes, Louise I., 1953–
    ML38.W66W62 2011
    781.66078'74735--dc23
                                        2011024561

Printed in the United States of America
1 2 3 4 5 6 7 15 14 13 12 11

CONTENTS

Foreword   1

Introduction   4

World Map   11

CHAPTER **1**   Historical Background on Woodstock

1. Woodstock Music and Art Fair 1969:
   Three Days of Peace and Music   15
   Douglas Cooke

   In the summer of 1969, nearly half a million
   young people gathered on a farm in upstate
   New York to listen to a historic collection of
   American and British musicians. A music and
   social analyst discusses the origins and legacy
   of Woodstock, which has become part of
   America's cultural vocabulary and the symbol
   of a generation.

2. Woodstock's Unconventional Festival
   Security   30
   *Wes Pomeroy, Stanley Goldstein, Michael
       Lang, and Lee Blumer*

   An oral historian interviews the people who
   developed the security strategy that helped
   make Woodstock a peaceful event. Festival
   producers did not want an armed force and
   hired a progressive police officer who agreed
   with their security philosophy and a community activist familiar with managing current
   social tensions.

3. The Festival Site Moves to Max
   Yasgur's Farm   45
   Michael Lang

   One of Woodstock's producers explains how,
   within days of city leaders banning the music
   festival from the original site, he found a new,
   more idyllic location. He describes the dairy
   farmer who leased them the land and helped
   them get local approval for the event.

4. Woodstock as a Coming-Out Party
   for Hippies   58
   Steve Lerner

   A journalist from an ultraliberal New York
   newspaper describes the festival and the
   people who attended. Drugs and nudity were
   commonplace. But despite the intolerable
   conditions, the hippies from across the nation
   who gathered at the festival conducted themselves better than expected.

5. Dire Prophecies Before, and High
   Spirits During, Woodstock   67
   Alistair Cooke

   A British journalist reporting from New York
   explains that despite dire predictions of riots,
   the young people who attended the festival
   enjoyed the music and behaved well. The
   locals were nevertheless happy to see them
   leave as they would any invading army.

6. The Impact of Weather on the
   Woodstock Festival   72
   Sean Potter

   A meteorologist explains how rain prevented
   planners from erecting ticket booths and

fences in time to limit entrance to the festival site to ticket holders. The rain also affected performances during the festival. While the rain brought some in the crowd together, others left early in misery.

CHAPTER 2   Controversies Surrounding Woodstock

1. The Woodstock Generation and Rock Music Are Dangerous to American Culture   **79**

   Wall Street Journal

   In an editorial published shortly after Woodstock, a conservative national newspaper argues that the hippie counterculture poses a serious threat to American culture. The widespread use of drugs and their orgiastic rock music reflected social and cultural decline, they claimed.

2. Woodstock Participants Were Peaceful and Community-Minded   **86**

   Barnard L. Collier

   A *New York Times* journalist reports from Woodstock that, despite widespread drug use, poor sanitation, a lack of food and water, and the need for additional doctors and security, the young festivalgoers behaved well and kept the peace.

3. Woodstock Planted Seeds of Activism That Persist Today   **94**

   Stephen Dalton

   Based on his interviews with Woodstock producers and performers, a British journalist asserts that the seeds of the social and environmental movements were planted at the festival. Current green and organic movements evolved from counterculture philosophies, and the hippies' peace movement continues to flourish.

4. The Fans at Woodstock Were Outcasts Looking for Belonging   102

Joseph Sobran

A conservative commentator claims that Woodstock was not a cultural milestone but a gathering of conformists looking for like-minded people. Wearing the same clothes and speaking similar slang, hippies were hardly rebels, he says. Moreover, free love and drug use do not solve social and personal problems but create them.

5. Some Festivalgoers Continue to Promote the Ideals of the Woodstock Generation   111

Paul Lieberman

An investigative reporter maintains that he and his fellow social activists, who bought a secondhand bus to travel together to Woodstock, continue their activism today. He tells their Woodstock story and explains what he and his fellow "pilgrims" are doing today to make the world a better place.

6. The Woodstock Festival Is Now More Myth than Reality   122

Jacob Bernstein

The media created Woodstock's mythology after the fact, claims a business and fashion-marketing journalist. At the time, the media did not anticipate the enormity of the event.

As a result, the media have unjustly privileged the Woodstock generation's history, which has effectively trivialized the experience for future generations.

7. Woodstock Was More Complex than the Myth to Which It Has Been Reduced   **129**

Maurice Isserman

A history professor and Woodstock veteran argues that Woodstock was not a time of innocence. It reflected the upheaval of the 1960s, in which young people fought for civil rights and opposed the Vietnam War. Woodstock, in fact, inspired many to participate in the mass demonstrations that followed.

8. The Woodstock Festival Site Has Historical and Cultural Significance Worth Commemorating   **138**

Michael William Doyle

A history professor claims that Woodstock represents a significant event in US history. An impressive gathering of rock musicians performed, and the young people attending were peaceful, despite the terrible conditions. Now part of the cultural vocabulary, Woodstock symbolizes the counterculture movement of the 1960s and is thus worth commemorating.

9. Views on the Legacy of Woodstock Vary Significantly   **151**

Jerry Shriver

A music critic asserts that among people polled by a national newsmagazine, views on the legacy of Woodstock vary. Some claim it was a paradise that inspired change. Others argue it was an epic disaster that reflected the hedonism of a generation. Still others maintain that Woodstock was simply a way to make money.

10. Advertisers Use Woodstock Nostalgia to Target Baby Boomers   **159**

Amy Jacques

The editor of a public relations magazine explains that parallels between the uncertainties of 1969 and 2009 have prompted some to market Woodstock nostalgia to baby boomers—the generation that attended Woodstock. Some think this tactic is harmless, but in the eyes of others, rebranding Woodstock diminishes its significance.

11. The Spontaneity of Woodstock Cannot Be Reproduced   **167**

Jason Laure

A freelance photojournalist and Woodstock veteran claims that at the time no one knew the festival would become a milestone of the era. Efforts to reproduce Woodstock have been unsuccessful because no amount of planning can duplicate its spontaneity.

12. The Woodstock 1994 Festival Reflects Cultural Changes   **171**

Stephen Rodrick

Using satire to compare the cultures of 1969 and 1994, an investigative journalist argues that Woodstock 1994 bore no similarity to Woodstock 1969. Outrageous prices and mass commercialization dominated the latter event, where the audience behaved more like terrorists than hippies, he says.

CHAPTER 3   Personal Narratives

1. A Woman Shares Her Woodstock
   Experience as a Teen   **177**
   Susan Reynolds
   A journalist describes how her Woodstock
   experience as a teen changed her worldview.
   United by antiwar sentiment and music, she
   and the other young people at Woodstock
   believed they could make a difference. After
   Woodstock she actively opposed the Vietnam
   War and became a reporter.

2. A Woodstock Musician Recounts the
   Experience   **184**
   David Crosby
   Admittedly high on marijuana, a Woodstock
   musician describes the atmosphere of goodwill amid all of the mud. He admits that he
   and the rest of the group were a little afraid
   before their star-making performance, because
   they were trying a new sound in front of fellow musicians that they greatly respected.

3. A French Visitor Recalls His Favorite
   Woodstock Moments   **190**
   Francis Dumaurier
   A French student shares his Woodstock experience on his first trip to the United States. He
   reveals many magical musical moments, his
   feeling of being among kindred spirits, and
   his pride at having been part of an event so
   momentous it can never be duplicated.

4. A Photographer and His Subjects
   Recall an Iconic Woodstock Moment   **194**
   Timothy Dumas

Quoting the embracing couple and the photographer, an art writer relates the events that
led to the famous photo that appears on the
cover of the Woodstock sound track album.

5. A Woodstock Festivalgoer Explains Why
   the Experience Cannot Be Reproduced   **199**
   Pip Klein

   A business journal publisher and Woodstock
   veteran compares her 1969 experience to
   a 1998 commemorative concert. Although
   much about her life and American culture
   has changed, she still enjoys reminiscing
   about her Woodstock experience.

Chronology   **204**

For Further Reading   **213**

Index   **217**

FOREWORD

"History cannot give us a program for the future, but it can give us a fuller understanding of ourselves, and of our common humanity, so that we can better face the future."

—Robert Penn Warren,
American poet and novelist

The history of each nation is punctuated by momentous events that represent turning points for that nation, with an impact felt far beyond its borders. These events—displaying the full range of human capabilities, from violence, greed, and ignorance to heroism, courage, and strength—are nearly always complicated and multifaceted. Any student of history faces the challenge of grasping the many strands that constitute such world-changing events as wars, social movements, and environmental disasters. But understanding these significant historic events can be enhanced by exposure to a variety of perspectives, whether of people involved intimately or of ones observing from a distance of miles or years. Understanding can also be increased by learning about the controversies surrounding such events and exploring hot-button issues from multiple angles. Finally, true understanding of important historic events involves knowledge of the events' human impact—of the ways such events affected people in their everyday lives—all over the world.

Perspectives on Modern World History examines global historic events from the twentieth-century onward by presenting analysis and observation from numerous vantage points. Each volume offers high school, early college level, and general interest readers a thematically

1

arranged anthology of previously published materials that address a major historical event, with an emphasis on international coverage. Each volume opens with background information on the event, then presents the controversies surrounding that event, and concludes with first-person narratives from people who lived through the event or were affected by it. By providing primary sources from the time of the event, as well as relevant commentary surrounding the event, this series can be used to inform debate, help develop critical thinking skills, increase global awareness, and enhance an understanding of international perspectives on history.

Material in each volume is selected from a diverse range of sources, including journals, magazines, newspapers, nonfiction books, personal narratives, speeches, congressional testimony, government documents, pamphlets, organization newsletters, and position papers. Articles taken from these sources are carefully edited and introduced to provide context and background. Each volume of Perspectives on Modern World History includes an array of views on events of global significance. Much of the material comes from international sources and from US sources that provide extensive international coverage.

Each volume in the Perspectives on Modern World History series also includes:

- A full-color **world map**, offering context and geographic perspective.
- An annotated **table of contents** that provides a brief summary of each essay in the volume.
- An **introduction** specific to the volume topic.
- For each viewpoint, a brief **introduction** that has notes about the author and source of the viewpoint, and that provides a summary of its main points.
- Full-color **charts**, **graphs**, **maps**, and other visual

representations.

- Informational **sidebars** that explore the lives of key individuals, give background on historical events, or explain scientific or technical concepts.
- A **glossary** that defines key terms, as needed.
- A **chronology** of important dates preceding, during, and immediately following the event.
- A **bibliography** of additional books, periodicals, and websites for further research.
- A comprehensive **subject index** that offers access to people, places, and events cited in the text.

Perspectives on Modern World History is designed for a broad spectrum of readers who want to learn more about not only history but also current events, political science, government, international relations, and sociology—students doing research for class assignments or debates, teachers and faculty seeking to supplement course materials, and others wanting to improve their understanding of history. Each volume of Perspectives on Modern World History is designed to illuminate a complicated event, to spark debate, and to show the human perspective behind the world's most significant happenings of recent decades.

INTRODUCTION

The Woodstock Music and Art Fair, held on dairy farm in upstate New York on a rainy August weekend in 1969, has come to symbolize much more than a memorable rock concert. For many, Woodstock has come to represent the ideals of the counterculture movement of the 1960s and perhaps of a whole generation. Between Friday, August 15, and Monday, August 18, 1969, nearly half a million young people from across the United States traveled to Max Yasgur's dairy farm in Bethel to listen to some of the most influential musical artists of the decade—as well as some unknowns whose performances at Woodstock would make them stars. The sixties had at times been a violent decade. Violence erupted at the 1968 Democratic National Convention in Chicago and at civil and student rights demonstrations. Despite unprecedented and unexpected attendance, food shortages, poor sanitation, and rain, the event was peaceful. Yasgur remarked to the crowd of young people gathered at Woodstock on August 17, 1969, "The important thing that you've proven to the world is that . . . a half million young people can get together and have three days of fun and music and have nothing but fun and music, and I God Bless You for it!"[1]

Woodstock's place in cultural history is clear. But the fact that it has become such an iconic symbol of a generation is perplexing to many, especially considering that those who were part of the event—the promoters, workers, performers, and audience—tell conflicting stories. The recollection of those who were there has, in many cases, been colored by the prolific use of mind-altering drugs during the festival and, of course, by the passage of time. According to Pete Fornatale, a New York radio broadcaster and author, "In some respects, Woodstock is just as much of a mess today as Max Yasgur's farm was on that Monday morning when Jimi Hendrix played his final note. . . . There are still so many stories to tell, even after all of these years. And many of those stories contradict one another."[2]

Fornatale compares these contradictory Woodstock stories to Akira Kurosawa's 1950 film *Rashomon*, in which four individuals witness the same event yet describe it in four subjective and contradictory ways. What actually happened at Woodstock changes with the storyteller, and the truth is therefore elusive. Indeed, multiple perspectives—conflicting recollections of events before, during, and after the festival—have helped shape the event's meaning and its mythology.

One of the people associated with Woodstock who has reached near-mythic status is dairy farmer Max Yasgur. Yasgur leased his farm to the Woodstock promoters after the city of Wallkill, New York, the original festival site, banned the event a month before it was to take place. Yasgur's progressive views about the young people who attended the event made him so beloved that a bumper sticker appeared following Woodstock that advocated "Max Yasgur for President." The *New York Times* identified Yasgur in an August 17, 1969, headline as a "Farmer with Soul." While Yasgur is often portrayed as a progressive, the reality, like much of the Woodstock mythology, is more complex. Yasgur did not support the views of the counterculture movement. He was, in fact, a conservative Republican farmer who was making a business deal when he leased his property located just outside Bethel, New York. While he knew that the men with whom he was dealing planned to host a music festival, he had no idea what was about to happen that August 1969 weekend. In truth, to ensure that they would have a site for the festival, the promoters were not particularly forthcoming about the details.

As the festival neared and throngs of young people traveled to Bethel, Yasgur and his neighbors became concerned that the event would result in disaster. However, when Yasgur met the young people who came to listen to music in his field, he was amazed that, despite their appearance, they were polite, peaceful, and intelligent. When he heard that some of his neighbors were charging for water, he was furious. Although his attitude was unpopular at the time, he shared his positive view of these young people that some called hippies with anyone who would listen. However, Yasgur did not at the time oppose the Vietnam War. He did not approve of the hippie lifestyle. However, he did believe that whether or not one agreed with their politics, the young people and the musicians who performed at the festival had a right to express themselves. He felt strongly that freedom of expression and speech were freedoms worth fighting for.

The Academy Award-winning movie *Woodstock*, released in 1970, also contributed to Woodstock's meaning and mythology. While the movie contains very real images, performances, and interviews, the 172 hours of footage captured during the weekend would ultimately be cut to three and a half hours. As a result, the edited version of the event is only part of the story. For example, one of the stage announcements memorialized in the movie comes from John Morris, the Woodstock production manager who tells the audience, "It's a free concert from now on." Morris informs the audience that this decision will be costly for the promoters. He adds, "These people have it in their heads that your welfare is a hell of a lot more important . . . than the dollar." The benevolence attributed to the promoters in the movie is somewhat misleading. The festival was not meant to be a gift to the Woodstock generation. In fact, Michael Lang and Artie Kornfeld hoped to use the funds from the festival to open a music studio in the city of Woodstock, New York, a mecca for artists of the day. Their partners,

John Roberts and Joel Rosenman, formed Woodstock Ventures as an investment that they hoped would make money.

In truth, the festival was free because of exigent circumstances, not benevolence. The people of Wallkill, who in late July banned the festival from their city, made necessary the last minute move to Yasgur's farm. Rain made constructing fences difficult. Time ran out, the ticket booths were not in place, and people began to arrive several days before the event was scheduled to begin. The promoters did not choose to go millions of dollars in debt without vigorous debate. One of the Woodstock principals suggested that people be asked to leave, come back, and either pay or provide a ticket. Knowing the likely response when he was asked to eject thousands of people from the infield, famed comic activist Wavy Gravy responded, "Look, do you wanna have a good movie or a bad movie?"[3] The promoters nevertheless remained reluctant to continue the festival for a loss. According to Morris, when he told the promoters that New York governor Nelson Rockefeller's chief of staff wanted to send in the National Guard, they felt they had no choice but to make the concert free. The Woodstock promoters did not want trouble at a festival promoted as "Three Days of Peace and Music."

Shifting media attitudes toward Woodstock have also contributed to its meaning and its mythology. In fact, even the "establishment" press—as members of the counterculture would call newspapers such as the *New York Times*—changed its attitude literally overnight. At the time, many people feared the counterculture, particularly after the violence that erupted at the 1968 Democratic National Convention in Chicago. The mainstream media of the day held the view that hippies and their antiestablishment lifestyle posed a threat to American culture and painted a negative picture of Woodstock. Indeed, a *New York Times* editorial headline published on Monday, August 18, 1969, read "Nightmare in the Catskills." The *Times* compared the hippies who attended the festival to lemmings, concluding, "What kind of culture is it that can produce so colossal a mess?"[4]

Those working for the *Times* who had actually attended Woodstock were dumbfounded by this characterization of the crowd. After a threatened mutiny by these reporters, the tenor of the newspaper's reporting changed. The next day, on August 19, an editorial suggested instead that those who attended had a grander goal. The *Times* wrote, "It is hardly credible that they should have turned out in such vast numbers and endured, patiently and in good humor, the discomforts of mud, rain, hunger, and thirst solely to hear bands they could hear on recordings in the comfort of home. They came, it seems, to enjoy their own society, free to exult in a life style that is its own declaration of independence."[5] Some experts claim that Woodstock not only changed media attitudes toward the counterculture movement, it changed media attitudes towards popular culture. According to Kenneth A. Paulson, president of the Newseum and a founding editor of *USA Today*, "In 1969 *The New York Times* covered Woodstock as though they were anthropologists. They had to explain strange words like 'groove,' and 'rapping.' . . . But you know what? The journalism world got hip very quickly."[6] Paulson explains, "The news business went from barely covering rock 'n' roll to an explosion of coverage in the next year. By the time a review of the Woodstock movie came around, it was less a movie review than a statement of human purpose."[7] That the *Times* could be persuaded to shift its views so quickly reflects the almost immediate tension between Woodstock reality and Woodstock myth.

While the traditional press focused on what went wrong at the festival, the nontraditional press sounded its praises and began to identify Woodstock as a sociopolitical event. The editors of *Rolling Stone* painted Woodstock as an event that announced clearly to the establishment that the values of the counterculture would not be denied. They wrote, "Out of the mud and hunger and thirst, despite the rain and the end-of-the-world traffic jams, beyond the bad dope trips and the garish confusion, a new nation had emerged into the glare provided by the open-mouthed media."[8]

The event's promoters, however, dispute the claim that Woodstock was a sociopolitical event. While they did set up a location at the festival known as Movement City for countercultural activists to distribute literature, they did so under pressure. Activist Abbie Hoffman threatened to sabotage the event. Fornatale maintains, "There could be nothing worse for the promoters than the movement portraying Three Days of Peace and Music as an overly commercialized, capitalistic, soul-sucking venture."[9] The promoters' goal was to provide great music in a bucolic atmosphere. The counterculture connection was ancillary. Nevertheless, the Rolling Stone review and the Movement City compromise combined to create the perception that Woodstock was a countercultural event—a perception that remains very much a part of the Woodstock mythology.

Commentators continue to contest how Woodstock came about, what exactly happened those three days in August 1969, and how Woodstock should be remembered. Although many analysts recognize that Woodstock has become, as musician Graham Nash suggests, more myth than reality, the event continues to resonate, reflecting the power of the Woodstock mythology. Indeed, for many, what actually happened at Woodstock is less important than what it means. The authors in the following volume tell their stories and share their views on this unprecedented weekend in modern world history. Whether these views illuminate the reality or add to the mythology is indeed a matter of perspective.

Notes

1. Excerpted from speech before the crowd at Woodstock on August 17, 1969, from the film *Woodstock* (1970).
2. Pete Fornatale, *Back to the Garden: The Story of Woodstock*. New York: Touchstone, 2009.
3. Ibid.
4. "Nightmare in the Catskills," *New York Times*, August 18, 1969.
5. "Morning After in Bethel," *New York Times*, August 19, 1969.
6. Quoted in Joshua Brustein, "Woodstock in Newsprint," Arts Beat blog, *New York Times*, August 7, 2009.
7. Ibid.
8. Quoted in Fornatale (2009).
9. Ibid.

World Map

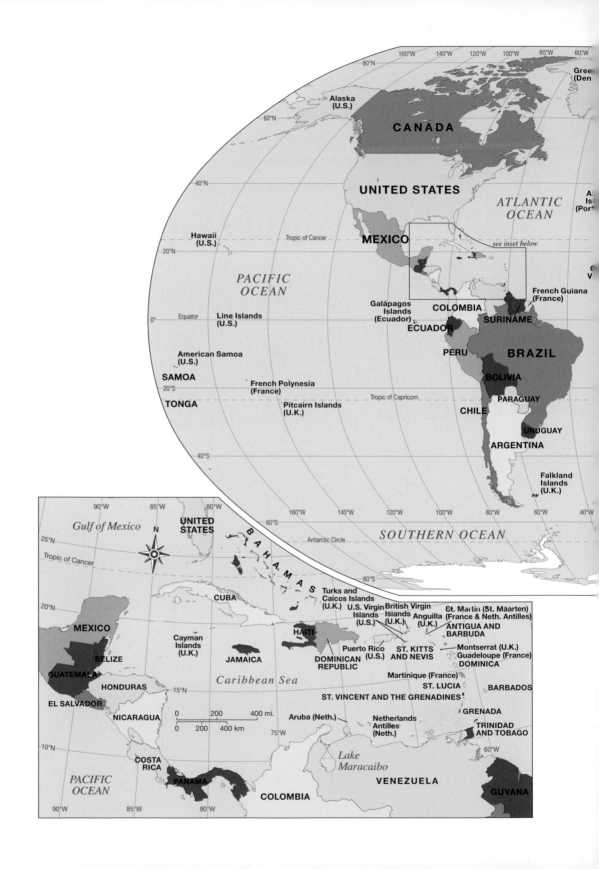

160°W   140°W   120°W   100°W   80°W   60°W

80°N

Gree
(Den

Alaska
(U.S.)

60°N

CANADA

UNITED STATES

ATLANTIC
OCEAN

A.
Is
(Por

40°N

Hawaii
(U.S.)

Tropic of Cancer

MEXICO

see inset below

20°N

French Guiana
(France)

PACIFIC
OCEAN

Galápagos
Islands
(Ecuador)

COLOMBIA

SURINAME

Equator   Line Islands
(U.S.)

ECUADOR

0°

PERU

BRAZIL

American Samoa
(U.S.)

BOLIVIA

SAMOA

French Polynesia
(France)

PARAGUAY

20°S

Tropic of Capricorn

TONGA

Pitcairn Islands
(U.K.)

CHILE

URUGUAY

ARGENTINA

40°S

Falkland
Islands
(U.K.)

160°W   140°W   120°W   100°W   80°W   40°W

60°S

SOUTHERN OCEAN

Antarctic Circle

80°S

90°W   85°W   80°W

UNITED
STATES

Gulf of Mexico

N

25°N

Tropic of Cancer

B
A
H
A
M
A
S

Turks and
Caicos Islands
(U.K.)

St. Martin (St. Maarten)
(France & Neth. Antilles)

CUBA

British Virgin
Islands
(U.K.)

U.S. Virgin
Islands
(U.S.)

Anguilla
(U.K.)

ANTIGUA AND
BARBUDA

20°N

MEXICO

Cayman
Islands
(U.K.)

HAITI

Puerto Rico
(U.S.)

ST. KITTS
AND NEVIS

Montserrat (U.K.)

Guadeloupe (France)

DOMINICA

BELIZE

JAMAICA

DOMINICAN
REPUBLIC

GUATEMALA

Caribbean Sea

Martinique (France)

HONDURAS

15°N

ST. LUCIA

BARBADOS

EL SALVADOR

ST. VINCENT AND THE GRENADINES

NICARAGUA

0   200   400 mi.

GRENADA

0   200   400 km

Aruba (Neth.)

Netherlands
Antilles
(Neth.)

TRINIDAD
AND TOBAGO

75°W

10°N

COSTA
RICA

Lake
Maracaibo

60°W

PACIFIC
OCEAN

PANAMA

VENEZUELA

GUYANA

COLOMBIA

90°W   85°W   80°W

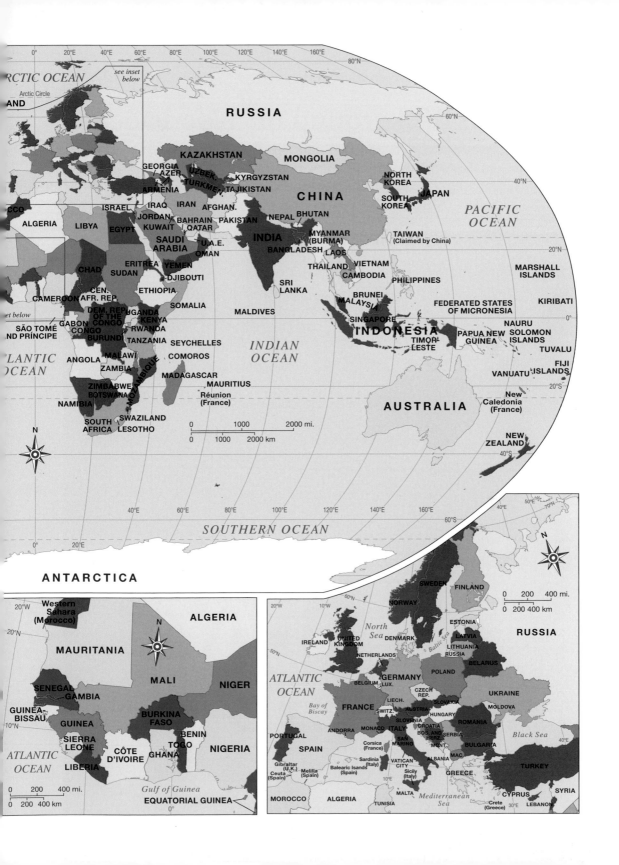

CHAPTER 1

Historical Background on Woodstock

Woodstock Music and Art Fair 1969: Three Days of Peace and Music

Douglas Cooke

The following viewpoint summarizes the origins of the Woodstock Music and Art Fair, the controversies surrounding the festival, and opinions concerning its impact. The young men who produced Woodstock booked the greatest collection of American and British bands ever to appear at one time and hoped to connect the festival to the 1960s counterculture movement. Security was unarmed, and a hippie commune maintained a free kitchen and tents for people on bad LSD acid trips. At the time, many saw Woodstock as a disaster. Producers were unprepared for the nearly 500,000 young people who came to the festival, which led to food shortages and poor sanitation. Moreover, bad weather turned the festival field into a sea of mud. However, later analysts claimed that the violence-free festival was the high point of an era racked with violence. Whether considered a disaster or an iconic moment, the memory of Woodstock has nevertheless become part of American

Photo on previous page: Artist Arnold Skolnick designed Woodstock's iconic promotional poster, which explicitly named the fair's themes of "peace & music." **(Getty Images.)**

SOURCE. Douglas Cooke, *St. James Encyclopedia of Popular Culture*, Belmont, CA: St. James Press, 2000. Copyright © 2000 Gale, a part of Cengage Learning, Inc. Reproduced by permission. www.cengage.com/permissions.

culture. Douglas Cooke is the author of several articles on music, literature, and social movements in the *St. James Encyclopedia of Popular Culture.*

In the 1960s, the small town of Woodstock, New York, 40 miles north of New York City, nourished a small but growing community of folk musicians including Bob Dylan, the Band, Tim Hardin, and John Sebastian. In 1969, Michael Lang, a young entrepreneur who had promoted the Miami Pop Festival the previous year, decided to open a recording studio for the burgeoning music community of Woodstock, which would double as a woodland retreat for recording artists from New York City. Lang pitched his idea to Artie Kornfeld, a young executive at Capitol Records, and Joel Rosenman and John Roberts, two young entrepreneurs interested in unconventional business propositions. Together they formed a corporation, Woodstock Ventures, to create the studio/retreat. They also decided to organize a Woodstock Music and Arts Fair to promote the opening of the studio.

> Most of the major American bands were involved in Woodstock. . . . The music soon eclipsed all other aspects of the festival.

As their festival plans grew in ambition, they realized that the small town of Woodstock could not accommodate such a festival, and a site in Wallkill, in the neighboring county, was chosen for the three-day weekend event. Throughout the summer of 1969 the project snowballed as more and more artists were signed to perform. It was decided that day one would feature folk-rock artists, day two would spotlight the burgeoning San Francisco scene, and day three would be saved for the hottest acts. By the time Jimi Hendrix was signed for $50,000, most of the major American bands were involved in Woodstock, as well as major British groups like the Who and Ten Years After.

The music soon eclipsed all other aspects of the festival, such as the arts fair (which is almost forgotten) and the recording studio (which never materialized).

Cultivating a Countercultural Image

Woodstock Ventures spared no expense to cultivate a hip, counterculture image for their three days of peace and music. They advertised the event through the underground press—which was rapidly mushrooming into a national network of anti-establishment groups—to put the word out on the street that this was the happening event of the summer. The Wallkill site was chosen for its rustic scenery and laid-back atmosphere, but the name Woodstock was retained to convey the bucolic theme of the event. . . .

Woodstock Ventures hired the Hog Farm, a New Mexico hippie commune, to prepare the festival campgrounds and maintain a free kitchen for those who could not afford to buy food. The Hog Farm also set up a bad [drug] trip shelter called the Big Pink for the inevitable freakouts that were expected. A group of Indian artists were flown in from Arizona to sell handicrafts. An impromptu organization called Food for Love was hired to run concession booths. Wes Pomeroy was enlisted as Security Chief. Pomeroy was renowned for his enlightened attitude towards youth and crowd control. He had witnessed the riots of the 1968 Chicago Democratic Convention, and had developed theories about peaceful crowd control. For Woodstock he organized a non-aggressive, non-uniformed, unarmed security team, the "Peace Service Corps," to unobtrusively dissuade undesirable behavior such as riots, vandalism, and theft, while overlooking non-violent activities such as drugs, sex, and nudity. New York City police officers were recruited, and had to undergo intensive screening to demonstrate their ability to understand and peacefully cope with young, hedonistic, anti-authoritarian crowds.

WOODSTOCK MUSICAL ARTIST LINEUP FRIDAY, AUGUST 15, 1969

Richie Havens

Country Joe McDonald

John Sebastian

Sweetwater

Bert Sommer

Tim Hardin

Ravi Shankar

Melanie

Arlo Guthrie

Joan Baez

Taken from: Pete Fornatale, *Back to the Garden: The Story of Woodstock*. New York: Touchstone, 2009.

Unfortunately, almost all these groups eventually betrayed Woodstock Ventures. The town of Wallkill voted to drive out the festival a month before the scheduled weekend, and a new site was found in Bethel, New York (although some townsfolk offered resistance there, too). The Hog Farm turned out to be opportunistic and irresponsible, stealing watches and wallets from the Woodstock staff and clashing with anyone whom they perceived as establishmentarian, including the medical staff. The radical activist and showman Abbie Hoffman, a self-styled "cultural revolutionary" who was charged with inciting riots at the Chicago Democratic Convention, threatened to sabotage the festival with his influence over the underground press if Woodstock Ventures did not pay him $50,000. He claimed that the promoters were growing rich off the people, and he felt that Woodstock should return the money to "the people" by financing his own political mission, including his mounting legal debts from the Chicago Seven Trial [a trial resulting from protests that took place in Chicago in 1968 at the Democratic National Convention]. Hoffman also threatened to put acid in the water. The Woodstock promoters knew that Hoffman had the audacity and the influence to arouse anti-establishment animosity toward the festival, and they paid him $10,000 to appease him. But such was the reactionary nature of the times that many radical papers nevertheless portrayed Woodstock as a capitalist venture promoted by "straights" trying to profit from "the people."

Betrayals grew more frequent as the festival grew nearer. The day before the festival, the New York City Police Commissioner refused his officers permission to work at Woodstock. The officers then offered their services anonymously under their own conditions, and for extortionary wages. Food for Love threatened to quit during the festival, reneging on their prepaid $75,000 contract. A rumor soon arose that Woodstock Ventures was bankrupt, and during the festival many bands demanded that they be paid in cash before performing. Even the Grateful Dead, the most anti-commercial band on the scene, made this demand (two years earlier they had played for free outside the Monterey Pop Festival). In the end even Mother Nature reneged her clemency, and assailed her hippie worshippers with two rainstorms, steeping the throng of 500,000 in mud.

> Many remember Woodstock primarily as a disaster . . . a monument to faulty planning, a testament to the limitations and hypocrisies of hippie idealism, a nightmare of absurdities ironies, and incongruities.

Remembering Woodstock

Many remember Woodstock primarily as a disaster, as it was officially pronounced, a monument to faulty planning, a testament to the limitations and hypocrisies of hippie idealism, a nightmare of absurdities, ironies, and incongruities. Over a million tickets were sold, but since the gates weren't built in time, droves of kids began streaming in days before the show, and by Friday the promoters, having no way to collect tickets, had to declare Woodstock a free concert. Acres of land that had been rented for parking remained empty as cars, vans, delivery vehicles, and an estimated one million kids clogged several miles of the New York State Thruway. State troopers arrested hippies on their way to the show, then danced naked on their patrol cars after drinking water laced with acid. Tons of supplies, and even some musicians, were

> Bad press, bad weather, bad trips, technical problems, human error, divine intervention—none of these pressures was enough to snuff the spirit of the crowd.

stuck in the traffic jam and never made it to the site. At the festival itself, a 40-foot trailer full of hot dogs rotted when refrigeration fuel ran out, and thousands of people endured the stench of rancid food while they went hungry. The revolving stage, designed to eliminate intermissions between acts, was the biggest and most expensive ever built, but once the equipment was loaded onto it, it wouldn't revolve (the only time it budged was when the mudslide moved it six inches). Out in the campgrounds, a "pharmacy district" developed in the middle of the woods, where one could shop for sundry drugs. Bethel residents witnessed outrageous acts of bohemianism. One neighbor awoke to find a shirtless girl riding his cow. Another found a couple having sex on his front porch. Meanwhile, thousands of disoriented hippies showed up in the quiet town of Woodstock, New York, looking for the Festival which was a county away.

Bad press, bad weather, bad trips, technical problems, human error, divine intervention—none of these pressures was enough to snuff the spirit of the crowd that had assembled for three days of peace and music. The most common feeling among all parties—producers, musicians, audience, town, and nation—was the sense of history in the making. It was the largest group of young people ever gathered, and the greatest roster of musicians ever assembled, and it became the defining moment of a generation. Initial media response tended toward panic, reporting the disastrous aspects of the event. But when riots failed to flare up, the media recanted, reporting that Woodstock was a peaceful event, a mass epiphany of good will and communal sharing.

On Sunday, Max Yasgur, the dairy farmer who rented his 600 acres to the festival, took the stage and

Photo on following page: A crowd listens to a performance by Richie Havens. Estimates of the size of the crowd at Woodstock vary from 250,000 to 500,000. (NY Daily News via Getty Images.)

complimented the crowd, observing how the festival proved that "half a million kids can get together and have three days of fun and music, and have nothing BUT fun and music." Of course, most of these kids were having a lot more than that, but the conspicuous absence Yasgur alluded to was violence. Rock festivals had become increasingly frequent since Monterey Pop in 1967, and each one was bigger and more riotous than the last. The assassinations of Martin Luther King, Jr. and Robert Kennedy also added a feeling of dread to any large gathering. When Woodstock promised nothing but disaster, then passed without a single act of violence, the relief that swept over the watching nation was almost intoxicating; it seemed like a miracle. The relief among the public and the evanescent bliss of the kids led to fanatical pronouncements of the dawning of the Age of Aquarius.

> When Woodstock promised nothing but disaster, then passed without a single act of violence, the relief that swept over the watching nation was almost intoxicating.

Bonding in the Face of Disaster

However, many commentators have since claimed that peace and good will arose not in spite of disaster but because of it. The hunger, rain, mud, and unserviced toilets conspired to create an adversity against which people could unite and bond. In "The Woodstock Wars," Hal Aspen observed that the communal spirit of Woodstock was typical of the group psychology of disasters: "What takes hold at the time is a humbling sense of togetherness . . . with those who shared the experience. What takes hold later is a privileged sense of apartness . . . from those who didn't." Aspen explained that the memory of Woodstock led a generation to arrogate "an epic and heroic youth culture" that subsequent generations could not match. Those who were once simply called baby boomers now dubbed themselves "Woodstock Nation," an independent and enlightened subculture. Abbie Hoffman wrote a book of editorials called *Woodstock Nation* immediately after the event, contrasting the newly united masses with the "Pig Nation" of mainstream America. . . .

It wasn't just the audience of hippies who bonded together in the face of disaster. Community and nation also rushed to their aid. The Red Cross, Girl Scouts, and Boy Scouts all donated food and supplies to the starving hordes. Even local townspeople pardoned the havoc wrought upon their town and made sandwiches for the infiltrators. The youths who had fled from their parents in pursuit of utopian visions ended up welcoming assistance from the very establishment that Woodstock symbolically rejected. They were led to appreciate that these groups had maintained efficiency to get them out of their jam. Someone, they realized, had to stay sober. Many Bethel residents, for their part, commented with surprise on the hippies' politeness and peaceful behavior. Mainstream America saw Max Yasgur's observation born out, that rock and violence were not inseparable, and that perhaps the peace the hippies advocated wasn't such a pipedream after all. In 1972 Woodstock Nation repaid the compliment by nominating Yasgur for president.

WOODSTOCK MUSICAL ARTIST LINEUP SATURDAY, AUGUST 16, 1969
Quill
The Keef Hartley Band
The Incredible String Band
Santana
Canned Heat
Mountain
Janis Joplin
Grateful Dead
Creedence Clearwater Revival
Sly Stone
The Who
Jefferson Airplane

Taken from: Pete Fornatale, *Back to the Garden: The Story of Woodstock.* New York: Touchstone, 2009.

The End of an Era

When the initial euphoria wore off it became common to view Woodstock not as the beginning of a new era

An Aquarian Exposition

From the outset, Woodstock's creators wanted to use countercultural images to promote the music festival. Since many young people equated the ideals of the counterculture movement with those of the astrological Age of Aquarius, one strategy was to call it "An Aquarian Exposition." Astrological ages are determined by the physical relation of the Earth to the stars of the twelve regions of the zodiac. Astrologers believe that these relationships influence human behavior. Although astrologers dispute whether the Age of Aquarius has begun, they generally agree on its characteristics and values, such as equality, freedom, humanitarianism, idealism, and rebellion—characteristics prized by the countercultural movement of the 1960s. Indeed, some believe the movement to be an indication of the dawning of the Aquarian age. While the original festival poster bore the stylized image of Aquarius, some among the promoters thought the image was too abstract. When the people of Wallkill, New York, banned the festival from its original site, the poster had to be redesigned quickly. While the words "An Aquarian Exposition" remained, the poster's designer, Arnold Skolnick, did not use the image of Aquarius. The final poster, a dove perched on the neck of a guitar, focused on the theme of peace and music.

but as an ending, the high-water mark of the 1960s, when hippie freakdom reached critical mass and dissipated into mainstream, and the establishment coopted the diluted attitudes and fashions into a commodity. Much of the pride and idealism of Woodstock Nation crumbled as the following years brought devastating casualties to their culture. Someone was stabbed at the Rolling Stones' free concert at Altamont in December of

1969; 1970 brought the student massacres at Kent Sate University, the breakup of the Beatles, and the deaths of Jimi Hendrix and Janis Joplin later that year. The following year, 1971, brought the death of Jim Morrison, the closing of the Fillmore Concert Halls, and the reelection of [President Richard] Nixon. Such defeats hastened the trend toward escapism, exemplified by rock's detour into country music and apolitical singer/songwriters, sinking into the quagmire of narcissistic spiritual odysseys in the "Me Decade."

In the wake of disillusion many claimed that the music was the most significant aspect of Woodstock, the only legacy successfully preserved. The documentary, *Woodstock: Three Days of Peace and Music* (1970), provided vicarious excitement for the millions who couldn't be there, and was enormously popular. It made innovative use of split-screen techniques to simulate the excitement of a live-performance, and won an Oscar for Best Documentary. The three-album soundtrack, *Woodstock: Music from the Original Soundtrack and More*, also awoke nostalgia for the swiftly vanishing epoch. However, the arrangement was jumbled, and many performers were omitted. A two-album sequel, *Woodstock Two*, provided more songs by the artists already favored, but there were still notable absences. For some people, the albums proved what they felt all along, that the music was only a minor part of what was really a spiritual event that couldn't be captured on vinyl. Janis Joplin and the Grateful Dead, who seemed to epitomize the youth culture that had sprouted in San Francisco, reportedly delivered lackluster performances, while then-unknown acts such as Santana and Joe Cocker proved to be among the highlights of the festival. A privileged few recall Joan Baez's performance at the free stage as

> Woodstock Two was a three-day concert with a ticket price of $135 (the original Woodstock tickets had been $18).

the highlight. The free stage had been built outside the festival fence so that those who did not have tickets could be entertained by amateur bands and open mic. But even after the festival was declared free and the fence was torn down, the ever-valiant Joan Baez, surveying the crowd of a half-million people, perceived that the free stage would still be useful for entertaining those who could not get close to the main stage, and she played to a fringe audience for 40 minutes until her manager summoned her to her scheduled gig at the main stage. This touching moment was not captured on film or record. . . .

The Anniversary Festivals

The most spectacular product of the 25th anniversary was the Woodstock Two festival in Saugerties, New York. As early as 1970 there were plans for sequels, but the original producers were in such legal and emotional disarray that it was impossible. For the tenth anniversary there had been an unspectacular sequel in New York City in 1979 with many of the original players, but nostalgia for 1960s flower-power was at low ebb at that time. But by the late 1980s and 1990s, nostalgia became almost clockwork, and in 1994 the sons and daughters of Woodstock Nation were ready to prove that they could party like their parents. Woodstock Two was a three-day concert with a ticket price of $135 (the original Woodstock tickets had been $18). It, too, generated a movie and soundtrack, and was broadcast on pay-per-view television. Woodstock Two featured mostly popular 1990s bands such as the Cranberries and Green Day, but also included older bands like Aerosmith, while Bob Dylan, the Woodstock, New York, resident who had missed the original festival, finally performed. Original Woodstock alumni included Joe Cocker and Crosby, Stills, and Nash [CSN]. However, CSN's presence did little to enhance the sequel's image. In 1969 CSN epitomized the 1960s spirit of togetherness with their angelic harmonies and intricate interplay of guitars. By 1994, they had sold "Teach Your Children" to a diaper commercial and consequently sold their respect. Woodstock Two also mixed rock and advertising, charging corporations a million dollars per billboard space. Pearl Jam, Neil Young, and others refused to participate for this reason. On the other hand, the promoters refused to accept alcohol and tobacco sponsors—a far cry from the pharmaceutical anarchy of the original Woodstock. The advertising slogan for the pay-per-view option was one of the worst ever conceived: "All you have to do to change the world is change the channel." The slogan alluded to John Lennon's line, "We all want to change the world," from the Beatles song "Revolution" (1968), which was very typical of the political preoccupations of late 1960s music. The idiotic Woodstock Two slogan reflected the apathy and passive consumption often associated with Generation X.

> "Woodstock Ventures retained its exclusive rights, but the memory of Woodstock nation belongs to the world; it is irrevocably imbedded in American culture."

The Woodstock Myths

However, one cannot blame the youth for the ineptly chosen phrase, nor assume that it reflected their attitude. The status of women, blacks, and gays was infinitely better in the 1990s than it had been in the 1960s. Beyond a few protest songs, Woodstock was a largely apolitical event. When Abbie Hoffman attempted to make a speech about marijuana reform, Pete Townshend swatted him off the stage. Many forget that the original Woodstock was quite commercial, as Hoffman and others had observed at the time. A common myth is that Woodstock was always a free concert, though it was only declared free by necessity. Hal Aspen notes that Woodstock is nostalgically eulogized as anti-commercial when in fact it was simply unsuccessfully commercial. Many of the

WOODSTOCK MUSICAL ARTIST LINEUP SUNDAY, AUGUST 17, 1969
Joe Cocker
Country Joe and the Fish
Ten Years After
The Band
Crosby, Stills, Nash and Young
Blood, Sweat and Tears
Johnny Winter
Paul Butterfield
Sha Na Na
Jimi Hendrix

Taken from: Pete Fornatale, *Back to the Garden: The Story of Woodstock*. New York: Touchstone, 2009.

innovations of Woodstock Two, such as the pay-per-view option, merely reflect improved technology and better planning rather than greater capitalism.

What really caused the Woodstock promoters to lose their credibility was their lawsuit against a simultaneous festival called Bethel '94 which was planned at the original Woodstock site in Bethel. The event was scheduled to include such veterans as Melanie, Country Joe McDonald, and Richie Havens. Woodstock Ventures, who had been thwarted and sued by many during the first Woodstock, launched an $80 million law suit to prevent Bethel '94 from happening. But 12,000 attended anyway, and Arlo Guthrie and others gave free impromptu performances. The litigation against Bethel '94 robbed Woodstock Two of any vestige of counterculture coolness.

Woodstock Ventures retained its exclusive rights, but the memory of Woodstock Nation belongs to the world; it is irrevocably imbedded in American culture. One of the most fertile legacies of Woodstock is the anecdotes, stories, and legends which recall the color and humor of that absurd decade. One elusive legend reports that a child was born, though no one seems to know whatever became of the child. The question usually comes up at anniversaries of the event, but remains a mystery. It is possible that the child born at Woodstock is simply a myth providing counterpoint to the deaths (there were three deaths at Woodstock: a youth died Saturday morning when a tractor ran over him as he slept in his sleeping bag; another died of a heroin overdose, and a third died of appendicitis). Besides the dozens of histories and memoirs, Woodstock has also inspired novels, stories, and songs. Its most famous anthem is Crosby, Stills, Nash, and Young's version of "Woodstock" from their album *Déja Vu* (1970). The song was penned by Joni Mitchell and also appears on her album *Ladies of the Canyon* (1970). Written in the style of a folk ballad, her song beautifully conveys the spirit—as well as the ironies—of Woodstock Nation, with its theme of pastoral escape, the rally of "half a million strong," the haunting subtext of Vietnam, and the poignantly passive dream of peace.

Woodstock's Unconventional Festival Security

Wes Pomeroy, Stanley Goldstein, Michael Lang, and Lee Blumer

The following viewpoint is an excerpt from an oral history of Woodstock based on face-to-face interviews conducted during 1988 by Joel Makower. It gives voice to those who developed Woodstock's unconventional security force. Stanley Goldstein was in charge of arranging security, in addition to many other responsibilities. He and concert promoter Michael Lang explain that the civil rights and antiwar movements created an "us versus them" mentality, and the police were "them." So that the event would be peaceful, Lang and Goldstein wanted an unarmed security force. They asked Wes Pomeroy, a Justice Department official in the President Lyndon Johnson administration, to head security for the festival. Pomeroy agreed with their philosophy and was considered an enlightened law enforcement officer. Lee Blumer, an energetic

---

SOURCE. Joel Makower, *Woodstock: The Oral History* [40th Anniversary Edition], Albany, NY: SUNY Press, 2009. Copyright © 2009 Joel Makower. Reproduced by permission of the State University of New York Press and the author.

and efficient former employee of music promoter Bill Graham, did much of the groundwork. All agreed that former priest and police officer Don Ganoung lent his experience as head of Christians for Social Action and his understanding of the dynamics of social interaction under stress, both of which proved invaluable to their security efforts.

Wes Pomeroy: In the summer of 1969, I had just recently left the federal government and started my own consulting business. And some guy named Stan [Goldstein] called me and said they were going to put on this rock festival and it was three days of peace and music and wanted to know if I would be interested in heading up the security. And I told him no. But I told him I would be willing to try to find someone who would.

There were several guys I had in mind, and they were all busy. One was John Fabbri, who was then chief of police in South San Francisco out in California, [who] later became chief of Fremont [California]. An extraordinary guy; he died about ten years ago. Another was Ben Clark, who I think is now retired as sheriff of Riverside County. He looks like a real tough guy, but has a marvelous holistic concept of where he is and where law enforcement ought to be, and of peacekeeping. I checked around and I couldn't find anyone I really trusted. And since I was recommending, I wanted to be sure.

Stanley Goldstein: I had asked a lot of questions of a lot of folks. I talked to some local police authorities and eventually worked my way around to the International Association of Chiefs of Police and had a talk with the head of the association, who gave me a list of names of people to contact. I was pretty direct in discussing what I felt were the criteria for the head of our public safety presence. In the meantime, I had worked my way through a lot of other possible sources. I talked to Pinkerton, talked to Burns, talked to all the private security agencies. I discovered who did security for conventions. Miami was a big convention town. I came from Miami, and I had certain contacts there. I contacted Rocky Pomerantz, the guy who was at that time the chief of police of Miami Beach. I pulled some other names out of the hat who were in the headlines. That was a time that there were conflicts all over and the names of chiefs of police were often in the news columns. Who managed conflicts? What towns didn't burn? You know, if it didn't burn, someone must have been doing something right. And if it did burn, how was that contained so it didn't spill and people weren't abused? It was library time and telephone call time.

> " We did not want to have any armed anything around, internally or externally. "

But there weren't very many folks to whom you could speak who could address the concepts and the concerns with which we were attempting to deal and the attitudes that we had. I must have interviewed personally fifty high-powered guys and cut that to ten or twelve, then reduced those to three or four to go further with, and presented to Michael [Lang] my conclusions.

The Woodstock Security Philosophy

Michael Lang: The philosophy in all areas was to get the best people available, people who carried the most weight in whatever their spot was. And who also understood what it was we were trying to do. In terms of finding a cop, it was sort of—I mean, those were pretty tricky times. And it had to be someone who had a good-guy credibility in the police world because we felt that less is more. We did not want to have any armed anything around, internally or externally. I went to every other big show in the country, and most of them had problems, and you could always see that there were confrontations set up. I mean, there was a squadron of guys with shields and bats and tear gas waiting to use them, and things like that went on. And it was kind of a game and everybody sort of got into the spirit of the game, and it wasn't really fun unless you got gassed. So I tried to arrange to avoid all that.

Wes Pomeroy: I was very interested in a couple of things. Most importantly was how they viewed the use of violence and control. I made sure that they didn't want security with guns and physical violence. And when I thought they were ready to do that, then I said, "O.K., I'll work with you because I believe in what you are trying to do." And I believe, generally anyway, that whether people act well towards each other or don't is a matter of a whole host of social contracts, most of them tacit, where they don't want to hurt one another, they don't want to victimize one another. I won't go into that; I can give you a whole philosophical treatise on that. But it's true. People see neighborhoods where there isn't a police car for days and there's no crime because people don't want to hurt each other.

Them and Us

Stanley Goldstein: This was 1969. We were in the middle of a war in Vietnam. We were in the middle of a civil rights revolution. The youngsters were—I use the term advisedly, youngsters—but there was a vast awakening of some kind of political action, I think inspired by the civil rights movement. The police were in general considered the enemy. *Pigs* was the common parlance for police. New York was a hotbed of social action and reaction. The Yippies[1] and the hippies and marches protesting the war, marches for civil rights, marches for gay rights, marches for women's rights, marches for the Pink Panthers and Black Panthers and White Panthers, and John Sinclair[2] was in jail for possessing two joints or

> [The police] were the enemies, the enforcers of all of these discarded attitudes.

something. Only months earlier, Lyndon Johnson had divested himself of the presidency and Robert Kennedy ran for president. Norman Mailer and Jimmy Breslin ran for mayor and president of the City Council of the City of New York, respectively. They had buttons printed, black buttons with white lettering that said NO MORE BULLSHIT. It was an exciting time. The world was in great flux.

There was conflict everywhere you looked—there was Them and Us. Vast assumptions were being made as to who Them were and who Us were, who represented "the People," and who those people were. And certainly the police didn't show a lot of hesitancy in using their billy clubs in trying to enforce the rules of society that were being rejected and overturned, willy-nilly. They were the enemies, the enforcers of all of these discarded attitudes.

It was obvious on the face of it that Woodstock was going to be a traffic problem if anything approaching the numbers of people or even a lot fewer were coming. There was going to be a traffic problem. And it was to some extent the telling argument with people who didn't wish to deal with police, who wanted to ignore the police, to find some other way. Cops stand on street corners in the middle of the worst weather in the world and wave their wands and point the traffic around. That's what they do. I don't know why they are willing to do that, what that commitment is, but they do that for low pay in the middle of all kinds of horrible, horrible circumstances. And you need to have some of those people around, folks that you can depend on. And so, since no one seemed to be able to suggest anyone else to do that, it had to be cops, or at least folks that had that kind of background and training, that had those kinds of discipline.

The Police and Civil Rights

Wes Pomeroy: I had been in law enforcement since 1942, twenty-seven years. I started as a California Highway Patrolman and had taken military leave in the Marine Corps for two and a half years during World War II. I came back to the Highway Patrol. After almost ten years I left the patrol and went to work for the San Mateo County Sheriff's Department, where they had a new sheriff and a reformed kind of an approach. I moved up through all the ranks. After eight years, I was the undersheriff, or the chief deputy in the county.

That was in 1960, when I became the undersheriff, and it was a great time and a great place. San Mateo County is and was a rich county. The politics, whether liberal or conservative—it didn't make much difference—people

The 1968 Democratic Convention in Chicago was wracked with the kind of violence typical during the late 1960s, which Woodstock organizers sought to avoid at the festival. (**Popperfoto/Getty Images.**)

had enough goodwill that they wanted to do good things. And so there were a lot of things going on. And of course, San Mateo County was the same as the rest of the United States in those years, and we had all kinds of challenges and opportunities and problems because of the emerging of a new reality in the civil rights movement. I've always felt, and I did then, that the police really ought to be at the forefront in that. They ought not to be dragged along by it. They're in a unique position in our society, and it's just essential that they be the leaders in what's happening out there.

[Comedian and social activist] Dick Gregory is a good friend of mine who put it so well then. He said, "If you're not careful, the cop is going to be the new n-----" because what happens is you get a school integration problem or housing or jobs, or whatever it is, and it's a problem of disenfranchised minorities trying to assert what they'd like to have. And then the police get involved because of the demonstrations and so forth. And if you're not careful, the clash between the police and the minorities—it becomes a police problem, which lets everybody off the hook, except the cops, who ought not be there in the first place. So what I said to people for years, whenever I had any influence over my commands, is, "Let's not let the Romans put us in the arena where you can't tell the Christians from the lions because it's not our beef. What we need to do is be more advocates with the people who we have so much in common with. We're out there with them twenty-four hours a day, seven days a week."

So that's what I'd done during my police career in the sixties. I was on a school board in a changing ethnic neighborhood. I was the president of a board that ran a halfway house for tough felons out of jail. The '64 Republican convention in San Francisco gave us a whole set of dynamics, and we ran that. Then Ramsey Clark offered me a job. He was attorney general under Lyndon

Johnson. And so I went to work for him as Special Assistant for Law Enforcement Coordination. I was able to take the job because I was a lawyer also; I'd gone to night school and gotten a law degree and passed the bar. I was appointed by Johnson at Ramsey's recommendation as one of the three men to head up the new Law Enforcement Assistance Administration. And we got that thing cranked up, and then [Richard] Nixon was elected [president]. In April of 1969, I resigned and started this consulting business, and that's where, several months later, I met the people involved in Woodstock.

Oh yes. In 1968, I was the advance person for the Justice Department and the coordinator for the federal presence at both national political conventions—the Republic convention in Miami and the Democratic one in Chicago.

A "Please" Force

Stanley Goldstein: I went down to Washington to visit Wes. I wanted to go to Washington anyway because I had been chasing again—sanitation and so forth. The Army knew about that stuff, and I wanted to get some advice from the Army about field conditions and how you keep from polluting water supplies.

Wes picked me up at Dulles Airport. I deliberately—well, this was a time [social and political activist] Abbie Hoffman had just been on television wearing a flag shirt and had been blanked out on the air and there was a big deal being made. And so I went out and purchased a shirt that was blue with white stars all over it, so that when I walked off the plane I would be able to see how Wes reacted. He just went on. He was very straightforward, very direct. The shirt didn't faze him.

> Instead of being a *police* force it was going to be a *Please* Force—a disciplined force that knew that a crowd of that size presents . . . a potential danger to itself.

I outlined what it was that we were doing. We had a relatively brief conversation there at the airport, and then he took me into town and we continued that conversation. Of all the people with whom I spoke, he was the one who most grasped the concept. He was the one who understood that we had a community-relations situation to deal with and that we needed someone who could be our face to the community who was not Michael Lang and who was not John Roberts [coproducer of Woodstock Ventures] and who could cover a lot of areas. And so it was immediately a structure and organization that made sense. Unlike others, he understood full well the concept of unarmed public safety and he didn't have any problems with that; that instead of being a *police* force it was going to be a *Please* Force—a disciplined force that knew that a crowd of that size presents, just by the sheer weight of numbers, a potential danger to itself.

Wes Pomeroy: Stan was this young man with—you get a sense of a lot of energy in him. I suspected he was idealistic, or at least espousing idealism. I always program for my natural, almost an instinctive, bias against New Yorkers. And I think I do it pretty successfully because if I didn't I wouldn't get through to a lot of decent folks. But Stan wasn't arrogant. And I thought it was an interesting idea. I just remember a lot of talking. I had to slow him down a little bit to make sure that I was understanding him. But it was a pleasant experience and I took him on face value and he meant what he said.

> [Wes Pomeroy's] concern and his perspective was that these were still kids and people and this was still America.

Stanley Goldstein: I think Wes was in his late forties, but very youthful. Stocky, strong, a good listener, and one who had the ability to zero in on important points, to discard the nonessentials, and get right to the heart of matters. I arranged for Wes to come up and meet Michael.

Mutual Respect

Wes Pomeroy: I met Lang and John and Joel [Rosenman]. [Artie] Kornfeld didn't seem to be much of a presence one way or the other. And I liked what I saw. I liked John and Joel right away. These were really interesting guys— idealistic, all that sort of thing. They were smart; they were intelligent. They had a lot of big ideas that didn't scare them and they thought they could do something. I thought, "Well, yeah, maybe they can." And I kind of liked them. You don't see people like that very often. And you never know if it's real. But they were willing to try. They had a lot of bucks they were willing to put behind it, apparently. I didn't know anything about the financing at that time. And Michael seemed to be someone that they all respected.

I don't know a damn thing about rock music. Well, a little bit. I traveled with Led Zeppelin after Woodstock. I was doing security. And it's not my kind of music, but I like music anyway and I get turned on by it. On that tour, the opening song was "Immigrant Song." When Robert Plant is starting off with that high-decibel thing and the whole place is shaking, I would be thrilled, too. But rock music is not my kind of music.

Michael Lang: I was surprised that someone who was working for Nixon, I think, at the time, would have such an open mind about the politics of the time. He seemed less concerned with being judgmental and more concerned with being prudent. And really, I thought that was the key for me. Not so much that he agreed with what our politics were or anything else. His concern and his perspective was that these were still kids and people and this was still America. And he was very cool. He had a good overview, a good perspective on things, and seemed to get a kick out of what we were doing and it seemed to be impossible anyway. And that seemed okay with him. I mean, it wasn't so okay with him, but at that point it was okay with him.

Wes Pomeroy: I trusted the people there. One thing that kind of struck me, because I never thought about it before, was how young everybody was. You get used to looking for talent and ability only in older people. Well, these people didn't seem to wait around for that. It was a very exciting kind of dynamic. But I was still—I resisted any effort to make me look like something else, either. I remember saying, "I am what I am. And that's a plus. You don't want to have a hippie security director. He's not going to be doing anything for you. I'm a policeman. I may be a liberal policeman, but I have respect in the field and that's going to be a lot of plus for you." It wasn't an issue really. I wasn't sure if it was, but I had kind of a hint that someone would think it funny to drop some acid and see the security chief freak out.

> "[Woodstock] would give [Wes Pomeroy] an opportunity to demonstrate some of what he really believed in terms of the way that police and community could interact."

I got the word out very clear: Don't do this; it wouldn't be funny. I wouldn't mind personally if we were in a big vacuum someplace, but it's not smart. Besides, there's a lot of money tied up in this and we don't want to risk it. I used the same argument about don't be smoking joints all over the place because some deputy sheriff will make his reputation by knocking this thing off.

Stanley Goldstein: I took Wes up to the Mills site and looked at roads. I think he was pretty much intrigued by what it was we were doing and what the attitude was as expressed by me, and wanted to do it. It would give him an opportunity to demonstrate some of what he really believed in terms of the way that police and the community could interact and relate to one another and what were the important and essential elements, and I think it offered an intriguing kind of challenge to him. Wes was not limited in his imagination. He could conceptualize and was intrigued.

An Effective Team

Wes Pomeroy: I was very comfortable in my role. They were comfortable in who I was and it was a very exciting thing to do.

I brought some people on board. I had Lee Blumer as my assistant, who was a very energetic and talented gal. They called her secretary. I didn't know anything about her except they said she had been a secretary to [music promoter] Bill Graham at the Fillmore East for about a year at least, and knew her business. She knew a lot of things I didn't know. They said, "Here is your secretary," and it turned out she was a highly talented person, knew a lot, and was able to function as a secretary very well. But she was more than that. She was just a damn good executive assistant. She had a phone in each ear. She did a lot of business on the phone; I don't know how she did it. And full of energy, a lot of hyper-energy.

Lee Blumer: They paid me two hundred dollars a week, which for 1969 was good money. I mean, it wasn't a fortune, but it was for a secretary, or whatever I was; I was never a secretary, because I couldn't type. But I was like some administrative assistant at that point. So, two hundred dollars a week, plus they were paying all the other expenses that we could supposedly invent. I mean, we didn't know that at the time, but that was what it worked out to be. I hate to say this, but they were paying for my Tampax. I mean, I didn't spend anything of my own money all summer.

Wes Pomeroy: I got John Fabbri to start giving his time at so much per day. He was a tremendously talented guy, and he did things well that I didn't do. I never bothered to learn all the technical aspects of some things that I need to have done because other people could do them. And he just was a very talented guy.

A Unique Character

I brought Don Ganoung on board, who was an Episcopal priest and I met him on the line at the '64 convention, because he was the head of the Christians for Social Action. We had become good friends and I trusted him. We called him an executive assistant. At the beginning, his role was to help us get permits. And he turned the collar around when he needed to, that sort of thing. And it was to give an air of respectability to what we were doing. Also, he had quite a background. Before he was in the priesthood he had been, I think, a warrant officer with a criminal justice bachelor's degree in the CID, the Army's Criminal Investigation Department, during Korea. So he had a lot of wide range, and he also had this ability to understand the holistic dynamic of social interaction under stressful conditions. He understood all of that. He was able to cut across at his priesthood ecumenical lines and other things. He was a humanist and a decent guy and smart.

> [Don Ganoung] was a priest and he was a cop and he kept going back and forth between these two professions.

Stanley Goldstein: Don was a unique character. He has since died at an early age of a heart attack. Don couldn't seem to decide where he properly belonged in life. He was a priest and he was a cop and he kept going back and forth between these two professions. He was an Episcopal priest and represented the church. I don't know the exact title, but the essence of it was ministering to youth and the disenfranchised—the Hispanic community, the black community. And he was a cop. He had been a cop for a while, then became a priest for a while, then he took a leave of absence from the church and became a cop for a while, and became a priest for a while.

Lee Blumer: Don was special. I'm really sorry Don's dead. We didn't know anybody else like Don that summer because Don had hung out with Bishop Pike, the Episcopal priest who later died in the desert; he was his administrator. And Bishop Pike was out there in another place. Pike was not your average Episcopal bishop; he was very metaphysical. And Don was defrocked somehow—he drank, he was defrocked; I don't know what happened. He may have told me and it was probably less significant than he thought it was, but it never stuck. But he gave it up and he never could forgive himself for giving it up. He really had a calling that he couldn't quite satisfy in the real world. We loved each other very much. I mean, we really came to love each other that summer. At one point I even entertained the notion that he should be my boyfriend, but that wasn't right. We just loved each other. Because we had just gotten so close; the experience was so, you know, forceful. And also, because he was so sad, and I'm so compelled towards tragedy. He just dragged me right in.

> We . . . were trying to get the physical lay of the land, how we were going to secure it. We were like cowboys.

Like Cowboys

Wes Pomeroy: I arrived in New York and went to the office we had near Greenwich Village before going up to the site. I think we were all a little uncomfortable with that first site. We were trying to make it something it wasn't, and John and Joel thought that there was an overpass that had to be completed or it was going to be a disaster.

And they had thought they knew people in Albany that were going to get that thing going and all cured and it would have helped a lot. But it still didn't feel right. I hear people talk about vibes and I don't talk about vibes, but I know it's the same thing. If it doesn't feel right and you're not comfortable with it, it's not right. I trust that kind of feeling I have in myself. But we started working.

Lee Blumer: I remember walking off the property—I was pacing the property to figure out maps. I mean, it was that kind of silly stuff. I was trying to figure out what the perimeters of the property looked like. We—Don and Wes and I—were trying to get the physical lay of the land, how we were going to secure it. We were like cowboys.

Notes

1. Yippies are members of the Youth International Party, a radical countercultural group known for a theatrical and humorous approach to political protests. It was founded by Abbie Hoffman and others.
2. Sinclair, a Detroit poet, was leader of the White Panther Party, a militantly anti-racist countercultural group of white socialists.

The Festival Site Moves to Max Yasgur's Farm

Michael Lang

The city of Wallkill, New York, the original site of Woodstock, passed a zoning ordinance that effectively banned the music festival. In the following excerpt from his book *The Road to Woodstock*, festival coproducer Michael Lang tells the story of how he discovered Max Yasgur's farm—the ultimate site of the festival. News traveled quickly that the festival needed a new site, and Eliot Tiber invited Lang to use his parent's motel in White Lake, a forlorn looking place that was quickly rejected. However, while driving around the area, Lang came upon a beatific farm with a field shaped perfectly for a concert. The next day Yasgur leased the land to Woodstock's producers for $50,000. Lang describes Yasgur as a sharp man who also was an eloquent advocate of the festival. In Lang's view, the bucolic location was much more appropriate to the festival theme than the industrial site in Wallkill, concluding that the rapid change of venue was a karmic event.

SOURCE. Michael Lang, *The Road to Woodstock*, New York, NY: HarperCollins, 2009. Copyright © 2009 by Michael Lang. All rights reserved. Reproduced by permission of HarperCollins Publishers Inc.

"I hesitate to think what will happen if the forty thousand people who've already bought tickets to our festival come to Wallkill and there is no event!"

"Is that a veiled threat?" comes a loud voice from the back of the packed room.

"There's nothing veiled about it!" I answer. "That's a problem that concerns all of us!"

A Hostile Crowd

Once again, I'm addressing a group of hostile Wallkill-ers.[1] It's July 14 [1969], and I want them to know that there might be consequences for them, as well as for us, if the festival is canceled. The anger in the room is so palpable I can't help but think back to what happened last month at the Denver Pop Festival when the cops and kids clashed. Like Denver, communications have broken down completely. I try to understand how we got here—how does fear become so entrenched that it squeezes out all possibility of discourse, logic, and fair play?

> How does fear become so entrenched that it squeezes out all possibility of discourse, logic, and fair play?

Two weeks earlier, on July 2, after five hours of debate, the town board approved the new ten-page law regulating assemblies of more than five thousand by a vote of 5–0. Slight modifications have been made, including lowering our newly required insurance bond from one million dollars to half a million dollars—and exempting the Orange County Fairgrounds (with its county fair and drag racing) from complying with the regulations.

Making a Case

We're appearing before the town Zoning Board of Appeals (ZBA) and making our case for the festival, after having been denied a building permit for the site. This is the same room where exactly three months earlier John [Roberts] and Joel [Rosenman] got the green light from the ZBA when they first proposed holding a music-and-arts fair at the Mills Industrial Park.

I've choreographed the presentation to impress the community with our competence and comprehensive planning. Mel, Stan, and Don[2] make articulate and convincing arguments. Stan reads a statement characterizing our festival as "a cultural event of major magnitude involving artists of all kinds, including painters, sculptors, filmmakers, and theatrical groups as well as musicians." He also states that we are committed "to preserve and enhance the pastoral atmosphere of the festival site."

Mel, armed with detailed maps, diagrams, and charts, explains that the site will be enclosed by chain-link and concrete-reinforced fencing, that an intricate system of roads and pathways is being prepared, and that in addition to the music, fine-arts exhibits, and crafts booths, there will be food concessions, medical facilities, campgrounds, portable toilets, and many of the things you might find at the county fair.

Don Ganoung goes into more detail about our security and traffic plans. He says that we're hiring more than four hundred security personnel, sixty mobile radio units, and parking lot and stage security guards. Parking facilities, he explains, will be located throughout adjoining areas where we've rented more land, and two hundred buses will transport concertgoers to the festival from the lots. "There will also be a screening process for troublemakers since no one will be allowed to drive to the festival grounds," Mel adds. "Some of our people will be stationed at the bus pickup stations to screen those who may be looking for trouble."

Then it's my turn. "We've already put more than five hundred thousand

> 'Generally the plans submitted are indefinite, vague, and uncertain. . . . The venture. . . . would be contrary to the health and safety of the public.'

into this project," I tell them. "We cannot get that money back. We are moving forward with this festival. Our work has been slowed by the circumstances of the past few weeks, but that's about to change. We are totally committed to the event, to the plans, and to the site."

An Ambush

My words are met with a loud and angry uproar. Being caught between two drawn pistols at Miami Pop comes to mind. I think to myself, It's definitely time to ramp up the effort to find another site.

The mood lightens in the room when the ZBA makes an announcement: Our field office—the barn next to the Mills property—is in violation of town zoning laws because we are operating a business in an area zoned residential. We have to shut down the office immediately. Following a big round of applause from the townspeople, the next announcement is just as bad. The ZBA will make its decision on our permit within forty-eight hours.

We're one month away from the festival, and we've ridden our horses into an ambush from which there is no escape. It's time to get the hell out of Dodge. . . .

D-day arrived on Tuesday, July 15: With none of us present, the ZBA released a four-page decision, REJECTING our application for a permit. The ruling stated: "Generally the plans submitted are indefinite, vague, and uncertain. Furthermore, the estimated number of persons attending has been too indefinite and uncertain, and based upon the amount and type of advertising, the venture would be contrary to the intent of the Zoning Ordinance. Problems of fire, police protection, and health would be contrary to the health and safety of the public."

Disbelief, shock, anger, frustration. From our field office, where he was packing boxes, Stan told a journalist: "There's a field out there, and come August fifteen, sixteen, and seventeen, there are going to be people out

Max Yasgur rented his dairy farm to festival organizers one month before the start date. (Time & Life Pictures/Getty Images.)

there listening to some boss sounds. If you ask me how we're going to do it, I don't know. But we're going to do it." . . .

Going into Overdrive

We had to find a new location for the festival—and fast. I knew morale would go down the tubes if I didn't refocus everyone into action immediately. I put anyone who was not packing up the site or office onto the phones to talk to press, local radio stations, Realtors, and others who might help us find a new home.

> *Penny Stallings*: Michael just went into overdrive to get the next space. Once it was determined it wasn't going to work in Wallkill, he was extremely reassuring that somehow this was going to happen.

All the ensuing radio coverage resulted in several phone calls coming in from people suggesting locations. Some were crackpots, but we checked out everything. The day after the verdict, on July 15, Ticia got a call in our Village office from a guy who said he had a place in Sullivan County that would be perfect for the festival.

> *Ticia Bernuth Agri*: When we lost the site, Michael told everybody, "Don't worry, we've got it under control!" He told me, "Ticia, you stay by the phones while I'm at the lawyer's office." He, John, Joel, and Artie were meeting with their attorney, Paul Marshall, to discuss their options. While he was gone, this guy called and said, "My name is Elliot Tiber and I've got land, and we want you in White Lake!" I said, "Oh yeah? We'll be right there!" I immediately called Michael, and in a few minutes he picked me up to head upstate.

Heading Upstate

As soon as I heard from Ticia, I called Mel and Stanley and told them to meet me at the address Ticia had been given for the El Monaco Motel in White Lake. My one perk from Woodstock Ventures—a '69 Porsche 912 I'd rented for the duration of the project—could make it to the location in about ninety minutes. Ticia and I zipped up the New York State Thruway to Route 17, followed it to Route 17B and County Road 52. Our Catskills destination—the Sullivan County township of Bethel—brought back memories of family vacations there when I was a kid.

Following Elliot's directions, we pulled up to one of the sorriest-looking motels I've ever seen. The sagging sign said EL MONACO, so we knew we were at the right place. A chubby guy in his early thirties bounded out to greet us, introducing himself as Elliot Tiber. I discovered that his real name is actually Eliyahu Teichberg and he grew up in Bensonhurst, right around the corner from me. He told us the motel belonged to his parents and that only a couple of its eighty rooms were occupied. . . .

On the way around the back of the motel, we passed all kinds of handmade signs on different run-down buildings named for various celebrities like Jerry Lewis and Elvis Presley. Scattered bungalows were caving in, and there was an empty swimming pool filled with debris. As we walked toward a sloping meadow, the ground felt soggy and springy under my boots. This did not bode well. . . .

"This isn't going to work at all." When we got back to the motel office, I asked Elliot, "Maybe there's someone who could show us around?"

"I'll call a friend of mine," Elliot offered, perking up after having looked pretty crestfallen. "He's in real estate." Stan departed, but Mel decided to go with Ticia and me. About a half hour later, a sleazy-looking guy named Morris Abraham arrived in a big Buick. He was happy to take us to check out some properties.

> "It was not lost on me that we had left *Wallkill* to arrive in *Bethel*— 'the House of God.'"

The House of God

A few miles from Elliot's, we drove along 17B through magnificent farmlands—it's absolutely beautiful farm country with open fields everywhere. We took a right turn off 17B onto Hurd Road. About a quarter mile up, we broached the top of a hill and there it was.

"STOP THE CAR!" I shouted, barely able to believe my eyes. It was the field of my dreams—what I had hoped for from the first. It was not lost on me that we had left Wallkill to arrive in Bethel—"the House of God." I left the car and walked into this perfect green bowl. There at its base was a rise just waiting for our stage. The others joined me. Mel, Ticia, and I exchanged looks of wonder. "Who does all this land belong to?" I asked Abraham.

"Max Yasgur," he replied. "He's the biggest dairy farmer in the county. He owns ten farms and two thousand acres. I can call him and see if he's interested in renting to you."

"Yes, let's do that," I said. I had to work hard at staying calm. I didn't want to appear too excited to this guy. We passed a sign that said HAPPY AVENUE, and drove until we got to a pay phone and Abraham reached Max. We drove on to his home—a simple white farmhouse—and met Miriam and Max Yasgur, a handsome couple in their late forties.

Getting to Know Max

"These people are interested in renting some of your land, Max, to put on a music festival," Abraham explained.

Max had a sharply intelligent face and looked me in the eye. "You're the people who lost your site in Wallkill, aren't you?" I was preparing for the worst when he added, "I think that you young folks were done a grave injustice over there. Yes, I'll show you my land—we might be able to strike a deal for your music fair."

Max got in the car with us and Morris told him we'd seen the field off Hurd Road and would like to start there. As we drove, Max pointed out some of the land he owned. My heart was beating so fast I hoped no one could hear it. We arrived back at the field and I told Ticia and Mel to wait in the car and keep Morris occupied while Max and I took a walk into what had become *home* in my mind.

"Max, can we talk about this field?" I asked. "This is the perfect place for us. It's the right size and shape and has great sight lines and great vibes." Something about the way Max carried himself told me to be completely candid with him: "It feels like we're meant to be here." I wanted to seal the deal right there in the field. We walked over the rise above the bowl.

"How much land would you say you'd need?" he asked.

"Well, in addition to this field and whatever you have surrounding it, we need another six hundred acres, including land for camping and parking," I told him.

"I still have a crop of alfalfa growing here and crops in several other fields as well," Max said. "How soon do you think you'd need them?"

"Would *now* be too soon?" I asked, with a smile.

A Sharp, Strong-Willed Man

Max laughed and pulled a pencil from the protector in his shirt pocket. He wet the tip of the pencil with his tongue and started to scribble numbers on a pad. A sharp guy, he figured how much he was going to lose on his crop and how much it would cost him to reseed the field. When he came up with a number for the bowl, it seemed a fair price and I said yes immediately. We agreed that he would calculate the other fields in much the same manner, taking into consideration whether or not he could harvest crops before we needed to prepare the ground. It

> Without Max Yasgur, there would have been no Woodstock.

was going to be a hefty sum, but I knew that this land was our Woodstock—and Max was our savior. As we shook hands, I realized for the first time that he had only three fingers on his right hand. But his grip was like iron. I was thinking, He's cleared this land himself.

Without Max Yasgur, there would have been no Woodstock. He was known in Sullivan County as a strong-willed man of his word. He had grown up on a farm with a boardinghouse where summer guests stayed. His father died when he was a teenager, so he became the head of the household. He'd studied real estate law at my alma mater, NYU, but his dream was to expand his family's property and create Yasgur's Dairy, the biggest milk producer in Sullivan County. He continued to buy up farms and land, building his dairy herd, until he reached his goal. He developed delivery routes and built a massive refrigeration complex and a pasteurization plant. All that hard work took its toll, though, and by the time we met him, Max had already suffered several heart attacks. An oxygen tank was kept handy for his use at all times, and he had an oxygen tent in his bedroom.

> Max [Yasgur] was willing to rent to us to give us a fair chance to accomplish our dream.

I called John and Joel to tell them the news: We were back in business—we had the perfect spot for the festival. John was guardedly optimistic on the phone but immediately agreed to come upstate the next day to work out the final arrangements with Max. I hoped he and Joel would recognize this for the miracle it was when they saw the land for themselves. I then called Artie and Joyce Mitchell and told them to let everyone know we had a home. I phoned Stan and told him to gather every set of plans we had and get back to Bethel ASAP. Mel returned to Wallkill to organize the move so the trucks could begin hauling everything on Monday.

The next day John and I met with Max, his son, Sam, who was a lawyer, and their banker. We had agreed on a $50,000 fee, plus another $75,000 to be held in escrow to cover any damages that might occur, and John had brought cashier's checks in that amount. After negotiating the other terms of the lease, including what we could and could not do to the land, we signed the papers at 10 P.M. that night. . . .

A Loyal Advocate

By Friday, July 17, it started hitting the papers that we were moving to White Lake. At first Max was a bit coy about it, telling the press that he was still deciding whether or not to rent us the land, but I knew Max's handshake was his bond. He was a man of integrity and an idealist. I don't believe the money alone was what motivated him. Max was willing to rent to us to give us a fair chance to accomplish our dream—much as he had done with the dairy. We showed him all our maps and detailed designs for Wallkill, and he was impressed by our diligence—this wasn't something just thrown together. He wanted to be paid for his land, but in return we also got his loyalty.

We still had to meet with the White Lake officials and get any necessary permits. After what we'd just been through, we were nervous about that. Max promised to help us as much as he could, and we had a preliminary meeting with Bethel town supervisor Daniel Amatucci over the weekend. He didn't think there would be a problem but set up a special meeting for us with the town board for Monday, July 21. We were moving as fast as we could. . . .

Landing on Earth

On Sunday, July 20, we took a break from our preparations for the town hall meeting to watch the lunar

> **"** America was putting a man on the moon, and we were just trying to land on *earth*. **"**

landing and see Neil Armstrong walk on the moon. The irony! America was putting a man on the moon, and we were just trying to land on *earth*.

Monday night, Don Ganoung, Mel, Stan, and I arrived to meet with town supervisor Dan Amatucci, the Bethel Town Board, and the Bethel Zoning Board. The room was tiny, and we all sat together around a table. Bethel residents showed up, but there was just enough space for a few to stand. Some peered through an open window.

Mel presented a hastily drawn plot plan for Max's land, which was filed with the zoning board. We identified the plot of land where we wished to hold the festival: three miles west of White Lake in a block bordered by Route 17B, Perry Road, Hurd Road, and West Shore Road.

We had hired a Sullivan County lawyer, Richard Gross, who told the board members that he had been advised by the Bethel town attorney Frederick Schadt that there were no zoning issues: Max's land was zoned commercial and agricultural. We promised to submit building plans as soon as possible for the board's approval.

Asking for Fair Play

Max spoke eloquently on our behalf, urging the boards to approve the festival: "All they are asking is fair play. Once we have formed a barrier against those who want to grow their hair long, we can just as well form a similar barrier against those who wear long coats or go to a different church."

"I would not stand in the way of anything if it is legal," Amatucci announced after our presentations. "We will welcome anyone to the town if they abide by the law, mind their p's

> Some sort of cosmic intervention . . . just hours after being expelled from Wallkill—had led us to a man like Max Yasgur and this perfect place.

and q's, and live within the law. If they do this, there will be no problem."

After three hours of discussion, we waited outside the town hall as votes were cast. While our fate was being sealed in that room, I sat alone on the building's steps, reflecting on what had to be some sort of cosmic intervention that—just hours after being expelled from Wallkill—had led us to a man like Max Yasgur and this perfect place. Coincidence or luck just did not explain it. It was karmic. We were meant to be here. As I looked up at the American flag waving from the portico over my head, I knew we would get the approvals we needed.

Both boards unanimously decided in our favor. Just after the meeting, Don Ganoung told the press: "They gave us the green light—the festival will be held as planned! We are all very excited. We have leaped the biggest hurdle anyone can imagine."

Notes

1. Walkillers are the citizens of Wallkill, New York, the original site that Woodstock producers leased for the music festival.
2. Mel Lawrence was director of operations, Stanley Goldstein served in several capacities for Woodstock Ventures, and Don Ganoung, a priest and former police officer, was involved in security for the festival.

Woodstock as a Coming-Out Party for Hippies

Steve Lerner

At the time of Woodstock, New York newspapers published conflicting reports of the event. While many newspapers wrote either detached reports or scathing commentary, the left-wing newspaper the *Village Voice* ran a front-page article that was more playful. A journalist describes the event as a pilgrimage for hippies hoping to confirm their lifestyle among others of their kind. Although drugs and nudity were commonplace, the stamina and tolerance required to endure the intolerable conditions that resulted from the large number of unanticipated concertgoers, torrential rain, and poor planning, proved that the young pilgrims were better behaved than expected. He quotes one departing festivalgoer's proud claim that the great numbers attending Woodstock prove that the "army" that demonstrated at the 1968 Democratic Convention in Chicago has grown. The author remains uncertain which event was the more revolutionary. Steve Lerner was a reporter for the *Village Voice*.

SOURCE. Steve Lerner, "The 10th Largest City in the United States," *Village Voice*, August 21, 1969. Reproduced by permission of the author.

The Aquarian Exposition at the Woodstock Music and Art Fair was fairly outrageous by anybody's standards. Stoned silly most of the time, more than half a million freaks from all over the country made the painful pilgrimage to Max Yasgur's 600-acre farm to play in the mud.

Although in the beginning the music was a good enough reason for the gathering at White Lake, after the drought, the famine, and the downpour one got the feeling that something larger was at stake.

> Many of the longhairs . . . were the only hippies on their block or in their hometown, and the mass rally served as a confirmation of their life style.

A Coming-Out Party

Indeed, most of the people who made the trip seemed to be looking for a kind of historic coming out party of the East Coast freak population. Many of the longhairs who walked up to 10 miles to the fair grounds after abandoning their cars were the only hippies on their block or in their hometown, and the mass rally served as a confirmation of their life style after months of sitting alone counting their psychedelic beads.

White Lake was an ordeal or an ecstatic adventure depending on whether you see the glass as half full or half empty. While the faint hearts will complain about the impossible traffic conditions, the lack of planning, sanitation, water, and food, and the general mismanagement of the fair, most of those who came accepted the insufferable conditions as part of the challenge of the outing.

Now if you can imagine a hip version of Jones Beach [a popular recreational location on New York's Long Island] transported to a war zone in Vietnam during the monsoon, maybe you'll catch a glimpse of what White Lake looked like a day after the long-haired troops occupied the area. The roads were hopelessly botched with no one to unsnarl them, cars moved more slowly than the endless columns of foot-weary refugees walking patiently for countless miles, while hovering helicopters ferrying rock groups in and out of the area made everyone feel as if they were out on patrol.

Perhaps most amazing was the physical stamina, tolerance, and good nature of a basically indoor, urban group of people caught in wretched outdoor conditions. It showed more dramatically than any planned demonstration could have that hip kids are fundamentally different from the beer-drinking, fist-fighting Fort Lauderdale crowds of yesteryear. At White Lake people shared what they had, overlooked their differences, kept their cool, and generally smiled all weekend.

The Local Reaction

From the beginning local residents tried to keep the kids off their land by lining up the whole family in beach chairs along the edge of the property to watch the parade go by, take pictures, and scream at anyone who tried to park a car or intrude. In the end, however, it was like trying to keep the locust off the land, and most of them gave in. Their woods became latrines, trash was scattered everywhere, ponds were used for bathing, and crops were stripped by hungry foragers. In retaliation a few of the local people started selling food and water at outrageous prices, but these were soon outnumbered by the more charitable members of the community, who started soup and sandwich kitchens in nearby Monticello and left the hose running on the front lawn.

By about 1 P.M. on Monday, Louis Foschiono, smoking a cigar and describing himself as a "well-known local resident," turned up at the trailer of the organizers of the fair to report that "Except for the traffic, all the local residents really liked the fair."

Rumor and Reality

Around Saturday afternoon, however, if one had listened to announcements from the one-acre stage in the middle of the fair grounds or to local radio stations, it sounded as if White Lake was the center of a disaster. Much of the talk about emergencies turned out to be either over-excitement, an effort to keep more people from coming into the area, or a plea from people who were already there to keep themselves together.

"Public nudity was also pretty cool, and by Saturday couples were swimming together in the lake without anyone stopping to gawk," reported the *Village Voice*. (Time & Life Pictures/Getty Images.)

Psychedelic Drugs, Counterculture, and Acid Rock

LSD [lysergic acid diethylamide] and other psychedelic drugs, such as psilocybin and peyote, came to occupy a prominent place in the youth culture that developed in the 1960s and continued into the 1970s.

One of the focal points for what became known as the "counterculture" was San Francisco, especially the city's Haight-Ashbury district. An area of traditionally low rent and bohemian lifestyle, "the Haight" attracted many young people who were in search of new experiences, whether chemical, sexual, or social. Although they sometimes referred to themselves as "flower children" or even "freaks," many adults began to use the term "hippie," a word that eventually grew so imprecise that it was often used to refer to anyone who looked, dressed, or acted unconventionally.

An important aspect of the scene was the music, especially the variety that became known as "psychedelic" music or "acid rock"—so named because listening to it could supposedly simulate the experience of a hallucinogenic "trip" without the use of chemicals. Psychedelic music was characterized by extremely high volume, deliberate electronic distortion, the use of synthesizers, extended instrumental improvisations or "jams," and the addition of Eastern instruments, such as the sitar, to the traditional rock instrument repertoire. The accompanying lyrics tended to emphasize mysticism or drug references. Some of the more successful acid rock bands included Jefferson Airplane, Iron Butterfly, Quicksilver Messenger Service, the Grateful Dead, and the British bands Pink Floyd and Led Zeppelin. Other musical groups, while not usually identified as psychedelic, sometimes recorded songs that fit the mold—such as the Beatles' "Lucy in the Sky with Diamonds," Strawberry Alarm Clock's "Incense and Peppermints," and The Jimi Hendrix Experience's "Purple Haze." Scottish folk singer Donovan had a hit record with "Mellow Yellow," which extolled the mind-altering properties of dried banana peels.

SOURCE. *Justin Gustainis, "Psychedelia,"* St. James Encyclopedia of Popular Culture, *vol. 4, ed. by Sara Pendergast and Tom Pendergast. Detroit: St. James Press, 2000, pp. 128–29.*

Rumors spread quickly predicting one kind of epidemic or another while in fact the problems of White Lake were those of any relatively large city. During the course of the weekend three people died (one was run over by a tractor by accident, another died from an overdose of heroin, while a third died from a burst appendix), three babies were born, dozens of miscarriages were reported, more than 400 people were treated for bad acid trips, around 4000 for minor injuries, and about 150 kids were busted—outside the fair grounds—for possession of narcotics.

The pink and white hospital tent near the principal helicopter landing area was a busy place for a while, with doctors treating cut feet and then putting plastic baggies around them so that the victim could walk the 10 miles back to his car without losing his bandages. One of the bearded doctors explained that most of the kids who came in on bad acid trips were just scared they had been poisoned, were suffering from minor stomach cramps, or in some of the younger cases just felt lonely.

> 'Do you realize that if we all stayed here we'd be the 10th largest city in the United States[?]'

Communications were difficult. The crowd was too large to find anyone in, and the loudspeaker was reserved for emergencies. Most calls for volunteers to help fix broken water pipes and sanitation systems were transmitted locally by word of mouth, but occasionally bizarre requests would be aired over the microphone: "Will Daisy Johnson please go to the Hog Farm kitchen? Sammy Cohen wants to marry you."

"Do you realize that if we all stayed here we'd be the 10th largest city in the United States," a 17-year-old blond boy wearing a chimney-sweep's cap and carrying a gallon jug of water suggested.

"Yeah, that would be far-out, man, but who would want to live here?" one of the few black kids who came out to the fair said as he surveyed the elbow-to-elbow crowd sitting on a hillside of mud and trash.

Bad Trips

Over the loudspeaker a scared voice warns the crowd that someone is selling poison tabs of flat blue acid and that there are already a number of people in the infirmary who are very sick as a result of having taken it.

"Wow, can you imagine what it's like to be tripping and hear that?" a tall girl with braids and a peasant shirt said to her neighbor.

Her neighbor, who was tripping, could well imagine what it was like and calculated that if one out of every 10 people had taken acid that afternoon—a conservative estimate—it would mean there were about 40,000 people spaced out in the immediate vicinity.

"If I caught that bastard passing out bad acid I'd make him eat all his own dope," a bug-eyed boy in a long black cape said flatly.

A few hours later Hugh Romney of the outlandish Santa Fe Hog Farm Commune got up on stage and invited anyone who was on a bummer to come up to their teepees and sit around and rap.

"That's almost worth a bad trip," a commune groupie said as she got up and headed off to find a hog.

"I've got acid here, mescaline, and hash," a dealer with shoulder-length dark hair called to the crowd he waded through like a popcorn salesman at a football stadium. No one was very worried about being busted in the middle of 400,000 freaks, and dealing was done out in the open.

Public nudity was also pretty cool, and by Saturday couples were swimming together in the lake without anyone stopping to gawk. In a way the nudity seemed more natural and necessary than fashionable, since everyone was constantly getting drenched in the rain and large numbers of people were wearing the only clothes they had with them. By Sunday, however, the bathers had gotten bolder and were sunning themselves on towels and petting each other as if it were the most natural thing in the world. By Monday a few couples were making it in public, guys were walking around with unembarrassed erections, and one unidentified young man was arrested walking home along the highway with no clothes on.

When Monday morning finally came it was gray and damp and everyone was huddled in soggy blankets. But up on stage Jimi Hendrix, wearing turquoise velvet pants, a studded turquoise belt, a gray suede fringed shirt with turquoise and white beading, a jade medallion on a pink headband, and a pastel tie-dyed leg scarf, played a mixed version of "The Star-Spangled Banner" and "Taps" and ended up with "Hey Joe" despite the audience request for Dylan's "All Along the Watchtower."

> When it was time to go, groups clustered around improvised signs for all the different states of the union to get rides home.

Heading Home

When it was time to go, groups clustered around improvised signs for all the different states of the union to get rides home, and even a hungry looking couple from Minot, North Dakota, found a car that was headed their way.

Like the Sinai Desert after the Egyptian retreat, the grounds of Max Yasgur's farm were covered with hundreds of pairs of ownerless shoes, a good 10,000 soggy sleeping bags, countless toothbrushes, and the stench that any large crowd leaves behind. In spite of the mess, Max was still convinced he'd done the right thing and received the longest, loudest standing ovation of the weekend from his guests.

Hare Krishna disciples with shaved heads, flowing robes, finger cymbals, and a vacant faraway look in their eyes weaved through the departing crowds passing out peacock feathers. And hard-working members of Students for a Democratic Society made their way from car to car along the congested highways trying to sell their copies of *New Left Notes.* They seemed to be meeting with little success.

"Hey, man, stop selling papers and join the revolution," an outrageous, toothless dope freak said from the tailgate of an overburdened station wagon when he was offered some radical literature. A girl with a fantastic magic marker design centered around her bare navel and a beautiful smile spread across her muddy face offered the vendor half a grapefruit.

A young man with red hair carrying a pair of broken sandals said as he watched the crowd leave, "It's incredible. Last year there were less than 10,000 of us in Chicago[1] and now look at this army." It's difficult to say which was the more revolutionary event.

Note

1. The speaker refers to the demonstrations at the 1968 Chicago Democratic Convention, during which rioters and protestors clashed with the Chicago police and Illinois National Guard over several chaotic days.

Dire Prophecies Before, and High Spirits During, Woodstock

Alistair Cooke

On the Monday following the Woodstock festival, the British newspaper the *Guardian* published this account from its New York-based US correspondent. Comparing Woodstock festivalgoers to troops that gathered at Gettysburg during the American Civil War, the author conveys the relief of the town's citizens when the festival was over. He reports, however, that the festivalgoers were well behaved. In fact, local fears of riots such as those that erupted at the 1968 Chicago Democratic Convention were unrealized. While drugs were clearly available, most of the young people simply enjoyed the music. His skepticism about the hippie lifestyle is nevertheless evident as he mocks one young woman's speech and refers to hippies as a different species. Alistair Cooke was a renowned journalist and broadcaster.

SOURCE. Alistair Cooke, "Grooving on the Sounds," *Guardian* [UK], August 18, 1969. Copyright © 1969 by Guardian News & Media Ltd. Reproduced by permission.

There was relief today when a camp-out involving twice the number of forces engaged in the Battle of Gettysberg [sic] broke out on the country town of Bethel, New York, and went home.

Over 300,000 hippies, rockers, pot people, and soul people converged over the weekend on 600 acres rented out to them for $50,000 by a dairy farmer who believes "we older people have to do more than we have done if the generation gap is to be closed".

Dire Prophecies

The occasion was something demurely called the Woodstock Music and Art Fair. It was, in fact, a pop festival, which the natives hoped would end all pop festivals. No prophecy was too dire for the residents of the small towns nearby, who feared that Farmer Yasgur was inviting on his neighbours a rural version of the [1968] Chicago Democratic Convention riots that appalled the country just one year ago.

There would be, he was told, wholesale pot smoking at best, heroin at worst, an ocean of garbage, universal bad manners, an orgy of love-ins, and probably a wild and bloody encounter with the police.

It was figured by the festival's young sponsors that 90 per cent of the nodding, swaying listeners were indeed "grooving on the sounds" with the help of marijuana. One youth died from an overdose of heroin and another was accidentally killed by a truck.

Two babies were safely delivered, and there were four known miscarriages. About eighty arrests were made without fuss on drug charges, and 400 were treated for "bad trips".

High Spirits and Good Behavior

But these casualties still left 296,000 or more in pretty good shape and incurable high spirits. The closest sizeable town is Monticello, and it had only 25 police, whose

Photo on following page: Members of the audience enjoy and play along with the festival's music. Dire predictions of violence and mayhem failed to materialize. (Time & Life Pictures/Getty Images.)

Jimi Hendrix: An Influential Rock Guitarist

Jimi Hendrix was born James Marshall Hendrix in Seattle. He taught himself to play by listening to blues recordings; left-handed, he used a re-strung right-handed guitar. He became known in the late 1960s for doing even stranger things with the instrument, such as playing it behind his back, playing it with his teeth, and setting it on fire. At times his stage pyromania overshadowed his musical pyrotechnics, but he is now recognized as perhaps the most influential rock guitarist in history.

Play Fast, Die Young

Hendrix began his career as a studio musician in the early 1960s and formed his own band in 1965. The following year he created a new band, the Jimi Hendrix Experience, and started to form a new sound, called acid rock, that employed intentional feed-back and

other deliberate distortions. His stage antics rather than his music gained him notoriety at the 1967 Monterey Pop Festival (captured on film in the cinema verité documentary *Monterey Pop*, 1968), but the band did have a Top 40 hit with their version of Bob Dylan's "All Along the Watchtower" in 1968. That year Hendrix directed his efforts to studio recordings, but he appeared with his new group, Band of Gypsies, in 1969 at Woodstock, where he gave a memorable performance of "The Star-Spangled Banner." He died from asphixiation resulting from a drug overdose the following year.

SOURCE. *Curtis Knight, "Jimi Hendrix, 1942–1970,"* American Decades, *Vol 7: 1960–1969, ed. by Judith S. Baughman, Victor Bondi, Richard Layman, Tandy McConnell, and Vincent Tompkins. Detroit: Gale, 2001.*

chief remarked at the end: "Notwithstanding the personality, the dress, and their ideas they were the most courteous, considerate, and well-behaved group of kids I have ever been in contact with."

After a day of heat and flapping wet winds, a storm broke and garbage came slithering down the hills like lava. The sponsors begged the thousands to take shelter. At last, however, the skies were washed clear and a quarter million or so of the undefeated gathered and smoked and cheered and rocked to Janis Joplin, Sly and the Family Stone, Credence Clear Water Revival, Jefferson Airplane, and other bizarre combinations.

By last night the hippies were high on rhetoric as well as pot. "A miracle of unification," cried one. "It was," echoed an eloquent female of the species, "like, well, you know, I mean, great, I mean beautiful, because even though the facilities were, like you know, bad, the kids and all were great."

The Impact of Weather on the Woodstock Festival

Sean Potter

The following article describes how the local weather influenced the Woodstock music festival. The area of the site had been flooded with rain in the weeks leading up to the festival, making it difficult for workers to complete the fence that would limit access to ticket holders. As a result, only one-third of the nearly half million who attended paid for admission. Although subsiding before the festival, the rain began anew on Friday, August 15, the first night of the festival, forcing four performances to end early. The rain continued on Saturday morning, but the weather began to clear in the late morning. The good weather did not last, however, and on Sunday morning a downpour turned the field into a "sea of mud." For some the weather created a common bond, but for others the rain brought only misery. Sean Potter is a meteorologist and science writer.

Photo on following page: While many festival attendees were emboldened by the rain and mud, some felt disappointed and dejected. (Time & Life Pictures/Getty Images.)

SOURCE. Sean Potter, "Retrospect: August 15–18, 1969," *Weatherwise*, July–August, 2007, p. 14–15. Reproduced by permission of Taylor & Francis Group, LLC, www.taylorandfrancis.com, and the author.

The summer of 1969 included several pivotal events that helped to shape the course of history, from the first humans setting foot on the moon to the first U.S. troop withdrawals from Vietnam. In the area of music and pop culture, the seminal event of the summer was the Woodstock Music & Art Fair, which has become known simply as "Woodstock," a name so iconic that it seems to define a generation. Billed as "An Aquarian Exposition" that promised "three days of peace and music," Woodstock was the largest of the outdoor music festivals that became popular in the late 1960s, the first of which was the Monterey International Pop Music Festival two years earlier.

The Impact of Heavy Rain

At Woodstock's peak, nearly 500,000 people packed the field of Max Yasgur's 600-acre dairy farm outside of Bethel, New York, about 50 miles southwest of the town of Woodstock, to hear musicians such as Joan Baez, Janis Joplin, and Jimi Hendrix. However, long before the first guitar pick struck a chord, the event suffered from weather-related problems. In the weeks leading up to the festival, the area around the site was inundated with heavy rain—more than nine inches in the month of July alone. On July 29, the town of Liberty, about 10 miles to the northeast, measured 4.33 inches of rain, the most ever recorded there on a single day in July. Because of the rain, Woodstock workers were unable to complete construction of a fence designed to ensure that only ticketholders were allowed access close to the stage. As a result, it was estimated that only about one third of those in attendance had actually paid the $7 (in 1969) price of admission.

> Woodstock workers were unable to complete construction of a fence designed to ensure that only ticketholders were allowed access.

The heavy rain preceding the event was merely a harbinger of what was to come. By 10 P.M. on Friday, August 15, it had begun to drizzle, and by about midnight the rain had become enough of a nuisance that the first night's performances ended 4 hours early, concluding with Joan Baez's version of "We Shall Overcome."

"Saturday brought continued rain, some despair, and greater crowds," read a line from a *New York Times* article about the event. "As the morning wore on, the weather cleared and good energy seemed to come with the sun." Despite the good energy, the sun didn't last. Barely an hour into the opening acts on Sunday afternoon, heavy downpours again disrupted the show and turned the field into a sea of mud that was ankle-deep in some places. The *Times* said people in the crowd began banging on metal cans while dancing and looking toward the sky chanting "Sun's Comin'," as if hoping to arouse some sort of sun god to save them. Somehow the downpours and deep mud seemed to create a common bond among those present. According to one account in the *Times*, "The strength of the crowd seemed strongest in the hard rain on Sunday afternoon. To the banging of the cans, dancing hippies gave all of themselves. Instead of despairing at the discomfort of rain and mud, the crowd rejoiced in its power to resist the weather."

> 'Instead of despairing at the discomfort of rain and mud, the crowd rejoiced in its power to resist the weather.'

Frustration with the Elements

But if weather can bring people together, it can also drive them apart. In an effort to give its readers a firsthand account of the Woodstock experience, staff members of the *New York Times* sat down "for an open, spontaneous discussion of the weekend in all its aspects" with several people who had attended the event. The following excerpt from that discussion relates the experience of three concertgoers (who were identified by first name only) and their frustration with the effect the elements had on their experience:

Jimmy: The main thing that broke it up was the weather. I mean, people got fed up walking around in the mud. It started to rain again on Sunday afternoon and we just looked around and said, "Forget it!" We decided to go back to our truck and decide there whether to change and come back to the concert.

Judy: We left the same way. We kept going down the road thinking, "Well, we can come back if it stops raining."

Bill: I didn't dry out from Friday night till Sunday afternoon. After the sun Sunday I was finally dry. Then along came Joe Cocker and the clouds. . . .

NYT: The Clouds? Are they a group? (Laughter.)

Bill: No, the rain clouds.

Beyond Woodstock

The same heavy rains that dampened both soil and spirits at Woodstock caused widespread power failures in northern New Jersey on Friday night and briefly halted service on one of New York City's subway lines. Meanwhile, some 1,500 miles away in the Gulf of Mexico, Hurricane Camille—the Katrina of its day—was heading toward the Mississippi coast. The storm made landfall around midnight Sunday night, just as the group Blood, Sweat & Tears took the stage. Camille, the second-most intense hurricane ever to make landfall on the U.S. mainland, lashed the coast with 190 mph winds and killed more than 250 people.

While several attempts were made to relive the Woodstock experience through subsequent concerts at or near the original site, they generally failed to capture the spirit of the original Woodstock. In at least one case, however, there were striking similarities; the 25th anniversary Woodstock '94 concert also experienced heavy downpours, prompting some to rename the event "Mudstock."

CHAPTER 2

Controversies Surrounding Woodstock

The Woodstock Generation and Rock Music Are Dangerous to American Culture

Wall Street Journal

During the 1960s, some American young people, who called themselves hippies, rebelled against the traditional values of their parents. In the following viewpoint written shortly after Woodstock, the editors of the conservative *Wall Street Journal* claim that the large number of hippies who attended the festival suggest that the movement poses a serious cultural threat. If these unkempt and drug-addled young people were to take positions of influence, the authors argue, the nation would not only regress culturally but politically. The authors assert that rock music is unrestrained and orgiastic and that Woodstock festivalgoers were wallowing in mud, both literally and figuratively. Even if social problems need to be addressed, "cultural squalor" is not the solution, they reason.

Photo on previous page: Woodstock took place on a farm in Bethel, New York. More than forty years after the event, the legacy of Woodstock—both the festival and the generation—are still being debated. **(Getty Images.)**

SOURCE. "By Squalor Possessed," *Wall Street Journal*, August 28, 1969. Reprinted with permission of The Wall Street Journal.

The so-called generation gap is not really so much a matter of age as it is a gap between more civilized and less civilized tastes. As such, it may be more serious, both culturally and politically, than it first appeared.

Starting with the relatively small hippie movement several years ago, the drug-sex-rock-squalor "culture" now permeates colleges and high schools. When 300,000 or 400,000 young people, most apparently from middle-class homes, can gather at a single rock festival in New York State, it is plainly a phenomenon of considerable size and significance.

> It would be a curious America if the unwashed, more or less permanently stoned on pot or LSD, were running very many things.

We would not want to exaggerate. Probably a goodly number will grow out of it, in the old-fashioned phrase. On campus, the anti-radicals seem to be gaining strength, and it may well be that these more conservative youngsters will be the people who will be moving America in the future.

A Culturally Poor America

But that prospect is by no means certain enough to encourage complacency. For various reasons it is being suggested that many rebels will not abandon their "life-styles" (the cliches in this field!) and that there are enough of them to assume some of the levers of power in the future American society. It would be a curious America if the unwashed, more or less permanently stoned on pot or LSD, were running very many things. Even if the trend merely continues among young people in the years ahead, it will be at best a culturally poorer America and maybe a politically degenerated America.

Now taste is that amorphous quality about which one is not supposed to dispute, so we won't argue whether rock is a debased form of music; we don't like it, but

Photo on following page: Festivalgoers relax and bathe in White Lake. Some commentators felt that the lifestyle exhibited at Woodstock, which included public nudity and sex, was a sign of moral and cultural decay. (Getty Images.)

Hippie Fashion: Rejection of the Establishment

As the 1960s moved forward, with them came a growing consciousness of social concerns, including civil rights issues and controversial U.S. intervention in Indochina. Many young people, disgusted with what they saw as rampant materialism and the moral failing of American society, found ways to separate themselves as completely as possible from the older generation—the establishment—that represented it. One of those ways was a revolution against traditional fashion values. The mods and the new youth market in general had simply rejected the older generation's clothing and its fashion choices. The youth of the late 1960s instead rejected established fashion of any kind—particularly anything worn or accepted by the establishment—in favor of their own unorthodox uniform.

The extreme of this revolution against fashion was found in the hippies or flower children. Sometimes with a vengeance these young men and women retreated from materialistic society, adhering to their own moral views. An important aspect of this rejection of the establishment was in the way the hippies dressed themselves. Flowers, the hippie symbol of brotherly love, were often worn in the hair, but they also appeared painted, embroidered, and sewn onto buttons, shirts, and pants. Bell-bottom jeans, faded and dusty, were the basis of the hippie wardrobe. Wearing a T-shirt as outerwear was revolutionary at first, but when that seemed too tame, they were dyed in bright strident colors; later they were tie-dyed in undulating, psychedelic spirals and circles. . .

never mind. Without pursuing that argument, it is possible, we think, to say a couple of things quite categorically about rock and related manifestations.

One is that a preference for a particular kind of music is not necessarily a matter of age. In times past many young people were drawn to classical music and retained that taste as they grew older. Today the young's addiction to rock is at the same time a rejection of classical and the more subdued types of popular music, and considering the way rock is presented it must be counted a step down on culture's ladder.

The establishment seemed much too materialistic, particularly when buying new clothes. In-stead of continuing that trend, hippies often patronized second-hand shops. They claimed they bought clothes for utilitarian purposes only, rejecting the traditional associations of clothing with status and taste. Army-navy surplus stores, Salvation Army stores, and other thrift-type stores were popular sources. Along with conventional views of clothing quality, traditional notions of gender-distinct clothing were also discarded. Sandals were worn everywhere by both men and women.

But going barefoot was preferred. Part of the antifashion movement was a move back to naturalness. So much of fashion seemed artificially restricting as well as symbolic of the establishment's unnatural rules of stylistic conformity.

The hippies moved toward an ideal of a more primitive, uncorrupted lifestyle. Hair was unkempt and usually grown long; young black men and women wore full Afro cuts. Young women wore little if any makeup. Going braless had been a radical choice for young women in the middle of the decade, but by the end of the 1960s it had become standard practice for some.

SOURCE. *Ellen Melinkoff, "Secondhand Clothes and Tie-dyed Shirts: Antifashion and the Hippie Influence," Judith S. Baughman, Victor Bondi, Richard Layman, Tandy McConnell, and Vincent Tompkins, eds.,* American Decades, *Vol 7: 1960– 1969. Detroit: Gale, 2001.*

A Disgusting Lifestyle

That is our second point: The orgiastic presentation on the part of some of the best-known groups. It is not prudish, we take it, to suggest that a certain amount of restraint is appropriate in these matters. But then, the whole "life-style" of many of the performers is incredible—disgusting or pitiful or both, but certainly hoggish.

The same applies to public sex in the audience, also in evidence at the mammoth Woodstock festival. It is not necessary to be a Puritan to say that such displays are regressive from the point of view of civilization. As for the ubiquitous drugs—well, we guess on that score we feel more sorry for the kids than anything else.

What perhaps gets us most is the infatuation with squalor, the slovenly clothes and the dirt; at Woodstock they were literally wallowing in mud. How anybody of any age can want that passes our understanding. Again, though, it's not a question of age. A person doesn't have to be young to be a hobo. He does, however, have to have certain tastes and values (or non-tastes and non-values) which are not generally regarded as being of a civilizing nature.

> Opting for physical, intellectual and cultural squalor seems an odd way to advance civilization.

Now we are aware of all the cant about how these young people are rejecting traditional tastes and values because society has bitterly disappointed them, and we would be the last to deny the faults in contemporary society. It is nonetheless true that their anarchic approach holds no hope at all.

A Confused Generation

They won't listen, but if they, and some of the unduly sympathetic adults around, would listen, here are some words worth hearing. They occur in a speech by Professor Lawrence Lee to a social fraternity at the University of Pittsburgh, quoted in *National Review*:

"You have been told, and you have come to believe, that you are the brightest of generations. . . . You are, rather, one of the most self-centered, self-pitying, confused generations. . . .

"The generation gap is one of the delusions of your generation—and to some men of my generation. . . . The only generation gap is that we have lived longer, we know more than you do from having lived, and we are so far ahead of you that it will take you a lifetime to have the same relative knowledge and wisdom. You had better learn from us while you can. . . .

"It is not mawkish to love one's country. The country, with all of its agony and all of its faults, is still the most generous and the most open society on the earth. . . . All generations need the help of all others. Ours is asking yours to be men rather than children, before some frightened tyrant with the aid of other frightened and ignorant men seeks to make all of us slaves in reaction to your irresponsibility."

In any event, opting for physical, intellectual and cultural squalor seems an odd way to advance civilization.

Woodstock Participants Were Peaceful and Community-Minded

Barnard L. Collier

The initial Woodstock headlines published in the *New York Times* reported disaster. Amidst the chaos, however, a sense of peace and calm emerged, which *Times* journalist Barnard L. Collier reports in the newspaper's Sunday August 17, 1969, edition. Collier asserts that the unexpected crowd of "about 300,000 young people" was well behaved, despite the lack of food and water and poor sanitation. Although he does report massive traffic jams and widespread drug use, Collier also quotes a police chief's surprise at the lack of misbehavior notwithstanding the size of the crowd. Additional medical doctors and security personnel were called to the scene, he maintains, and one commune handed out free food. In the end, Collier reports, festivalgoers heard plenty of music and "the peace was being kept."

SOURCE. Barnard L. Collier, "300,000 at Folk-Rock Fair Camp Out in a Sea of Mud," *New York Times*, August 17, 1969. Reproduced by permission of the author.

Despite massive traffic jams, drenching rainstorms and shortages of food, water and medical facilities, about 300,000 young people swarmed over this rural area today for the Woodstock Music and Art Fair.

Drawn by such performers as Joan Baez, Ravi Shankar, Jimi Hendrix and the Jefferson Airplane, the prospect of drugs and the excitement of "making the scene," the young people came in droves, camping in the woods, romping in the mud, talking, smoking and listening to the wailing music.

Looking out over 20 acres of youths squeezed body to body, the festival's organizers, the state police and officials of the Sullivan County Sheriff's office agreed that the crowd was over 300,000.

> Most of the hip, swinging youngsters heard the music on stage only as a distant rumble. It was almost impossible for them to tell who was performing.

Participants Well Behaved

The crowd, which camped on the 600-acre farm of Max Yasgur near here for the three-day festival, was well-behaved, according to both the sponsors and the police, even though about 75 persons is the area were arrested, mostly on charges of possessing narcotics.

Most of the hip, swinging youngsters heard the music on stage only as a distant rumble. It was almost impossible for them to tell who was performing and probably only about half the crowd could hear a note. Yet they stayed by the thousands, often standing ankle-deep in mud, sometimes paying enterprising peddlers 25 cents for a glass of water.

Roadways leading from the site were lined tonight with thousands of weary-looking youths who had had enough, and were trying to reach places where they could get food or transportation.

During the first 24 hours of the fair, festival medical officers said that a thousand people had been treated at first-aid stations for various ailments, including exposure and a few accident cases. About 300 were ill because of adverse drug reactions.

Doctors Fly to the Scene

A dozen doctors, responding to a plea from the fair's sponsors, flew from New York to the scene, about 70 miles northwest of the city, near the Catskill Mountain resorts of Liberty and Monticello.

Michael Lang, the 24-year-old producer of the event, said that the medical help was summoned not because of any widespread illnesses, but because of the potential threat of a virus cold or pneumonia epidemic among such a large gathering.

Parked cars jammed roadways in all directions for up to 20 miles, and thousands of festival-goers, weary after long walks to get here, had to spend the night sleeping on the rain-soaked ground. They awoke to find food and water shortages.

'It's about the quietest, most well-behaved 300,000 people in one place that can be imagined.'

But Mr. Lang said this afternoon: "It's about the quietest, most well-behaved 300,000 people in one place that can be imagined. There have been no fights or incidents of violence of any kind."

A state police official agreed. "I was dumfounded by the size of the crowd," he said. "I can hardly believe that there haven't been even small incidents of misbehavior by the young people."

Dr. Donald Goldecker, the fair's medical officer, said that most of those suffering from the ill effects of drugs had experienced "bad LSD trips." The symptoms are agitation, disorientation and fear, lasting three to four hours.

The fair's sponsors brought in 100 members of a group called the Hog Farm Commune of Santa Fe, N.M., who formerly used LSD, to act as security guards. They also attempted to treat "bad trips" with soothing, understanding talk and assurances that a sufferer is not dying or going insane.

Tonight, a festival announcer warned from the stage that "badly manufactured acid" [a term for LSD] was being circulated. He said:

"You aren't taking poison acid. The acid's not poison. It's just badly manufactured acid. You are not going to die. We have treated 300 cases and it's all just badly manufactured acid. So if you think you've taken poison, you haven't. But if you're worried, just take half a tablet."

As the crowd swelled today, officials of the fair issued an urgent appeal for all those not already at the muddy site to stay away.

It was impossible, they said, to get to the site without walking for miles. Parked and stalled cars were bumper-to-bumper for 20 miles in all directions on Routes 17, 17B, 42, 55 and 97.

Bus Service Canceled

The Short Line Bus Company, which has provided the only bus service to the festival from New York, said yesterday it was canceling all buses to the festival and Bethel at the request of the police. "We're not driving into that disaster area," a company spokesman said.

Yesterday, 65 buses from New York City went to the festival. One took 12 hours to get there, with the average running more than four hours. The customary travel time is two hours 20 minutes.

Despite the distance, columns of festival-goers were trudging on

> Those reaching the site found tens of thousands of tents, campers and makeshift lean-to shacks—some of them rather elaborate.

Onsite nurses and doctors provided medical care during the festival. Although there were three deaths, no incidents of violence or serious injury were reported. (Time & Life Pictures/Getty Images.)

the highways toward the site. Their lines stretched back three to four miles in the afternoon.

Those reaching the site found tens of thousands of tents, campers and makeshift lean-to shacks—some of them rather elaborate—made of any materials at hand, including trees, wood, ropes, sheets and blankets.

A Teepee for Twenty People

One such was constructed as a teepee around a big elm tree. It had a fire inside and a hole at the top for the smoke to pour out. About 20 persons slept inside the tent last night with their heads toward the fire, like the spokes of a wheel.

The first day's music was to have ended at 4 A.M. today, but because of the weather the performances were concluded shortly after midnight.

Joan Baez ended it for the night by leading the crowd in singing "We Shall Overcome." Afterward, she told the audience, "I hope David can hear it," referring to her husband, who is in jail for refusing to be drafted.

Today, thousands of fans, evidently discouraged by the weather and the press of the crowds, began leaving the festival site, which has turned into a giant mud puddle.

But they were quickly replaced by many more thousands seeking to get in.

Festival officials, unable to cope with the growing crowds, stopped selling tickets. "Now it's all a freebee," one said. The tickets had been sold for $7-day or $18 for the three-day weekend, which was scheduled to end tomorrow night.

Many of those leaving the festival today, encountering others just arriving on the roads outside the site, attempted to sell their weekend passes for money or food.

"Two tickets are worth a peach or half a sandwich," one departing youth said.

Festival officials today said they were sending representatives through the crowd seeking donations.

John Roberts, a 24-year-old officer of Woodstock Ventures, Inc., which sponsored the festival, said today that the organizers expected to lose money on the enterprise.

The organizers had expected 150,000 to 200,000 persons to attend, and conceded today that they were unprepared for the numbers that actually arrived.

Shortage of Food

Six water wells were dug on the site and 600 portable toilets brought in.

The festival was originally scheduled to be held at Woodstock, 50 miles northeast of here, but a suitable location there was not available. The sponsors then turned to Wallkill, about 30 miles south of Woodstock, but were rebuffed and finally decided on Mr. Yasgur's farm here.

> The members of one commune were passing out a free gruel of peanuts, oatmeal, raisins and sunflower seeds.

Many youths brought their own food, but there was a shortage at the concession stands set up around the festival site.

The members of one commune were passing out a free gruel of peanuts, oatmeal, raisins and sunflower seeds. Local farmers around the site complained to the police that corn and vegetables had been stripped in their fields by foragers.

Piles of garbage built up everywhere, and scores of men employed to collect it were hard pressed. . . .

Two Hundred in Security Force

Charged with keeping the peace was a 200-man "peace-security force," consisting of off-duty policemen from a number of communities as well as state troopers, off-duty state correction officers and Sullivan County Sheriff's deputies.

This afternoon, the festival promoters asked for more state policemen and aid from the Sullivan County Red Cross and Civil Defense organizations. The promoters said the reinforcements were being requested as a precautionary measure to help handle the large crowd and not because of any outbreaks of violence.

Additional sheriff's deputies also were brought from Dutchess, Saratoga and Rockland Counties.

In addition to a food shortage, festival officials said that a water shortage also was developing.

About 20 doctors and 50 nurses were on the site today before the arrival of the additional medical personnel. Some of the doctors said that the "bad LSD trips" had resulted from the circulation of some "flat blue acid tablets being passed around."

They also said tranquilizers were being peddled as LSD, which stands for lysergic acid diethylamide.

A state police sergeant said no one on the festival site was being arrested for the use of marijuana. "If we did [make such arrests], there isn't enough space in Sullivan or the next three counties to put them in," he said.

The music that brought the youngsters to the festival began last night with a folk orientation. Today's acts included the Who, the Jefferson Airplane and Janis Joplin. Tomorrow's billing included The Band, Jimi Hendrix, and Crosby, Stills and Nash.

The performers were at first ferried to the site by helicopter from an airport in nearby Liberty. But the promoters were forced to abandon this plan when most of the copters developed mechanical difficulties and the gasoline pumps at the airport ran dry. The theme of the festival was billed as "Peace and Music." There was plenty of music, and, according to the police, the peace was being kept.

Woodstock Planted Seeds of Activism that Persist Today

Stephen Dalton

In the viewpoint that follows, a British journalist reports that Woodstock planted the seeds of today's environmental and social movements, according to those who produced and performed at the festival. Woodstock producer Michael Lang says that the green and organic movements of today began at the time of Woodstock, and Michael Wadleigh, who directed the Oscar-winning documentary about the festival, is currently a sustainable development activist. Performer Country Joe McDonald says that the peace movement, traced back to Woodstock, was not a revolution to take over the United States, but to plant the seeds of hope during a dark period—not unlike the theme of hope that accompanied President Barack Obama's inauguration. Stephen Dalton is a British journalist and music critic whose writing has appeared in *New Music Express*, the *Times* of London, *Uncut*, *Scotland on Sunday*, and various other publications.

Photo on following page: Some contend that today's environmental movement sprouted from Woodstock's optimism and feeling of camaraderie. (**Washington Post/ Getty Images.**)

Forty years on, Woodstock is still dividing opinion. Pete Townshend recently described The Who's performance at this epoch-making hippy festival in 1969 as "the most important single concert that we ever did." But Roger Daltrey's verdict is harsher: "The worst gig we ever played."

Billed as "three days of peace and music," Woodstock took place on a hot midAugust weekend on rolling farmland in upstate New York. Half a million rock fans, freaks and hippies converged on the sleepy town of Bethel, jamming traffic for miles and overwhelming the organisers. On Friday afternoon they trampled the fences, turning Woodstock into a free festival.

An Idyllic Reputation

Consequently, it also became a notorious financial disaster. But Woodstock's idyllic reputation was sealed for ever by a best-selling soundtrack album and Michael Wadleigh's Oscar-winning documentary. Both became huge hits, saving Warner Brothers from bankruptcy. Released on DVD and Blu-ray, the digitally remastered 40th anniversary edition of Wadleigh's film offers a fantastic journey through Woodstock. It features classic sets from The Who, Jimi Hendrix, Janis Joplin, Joe Cocker, Joan Baez, Santana and more—including two extra hours of previously unseen archive performances.

'A lot of the seeds [of social movements] that have grown up today were planted [at the time of Woodstock].'

The Woodstock movie opens with beatific flower children cavorting in a sun-dappled agrarian idyll, but ends with weary lines of mud-caked refugees trudging away from a storm-lashed disaster area as Jimi Hendrix torches *The Star Spangled Banner*. A grand metaphor, perhaps, for the crash-and-burn arc of counterculture idealism. But if we look beyond the tie-dyed fashions and Vietnam references, much of Wadleigh's film looks uncannily like a contemporary Glastonbury or Bestival [annual musical festivals in Great Britain].

The Woodstock Nation Lives

The stoned innocence that fuelled Woodstock is easy to mock today, and many do. And yet everyone interviewed for this feature still belongs to the Woodstock nation to some degree. Now living on a farm in West Wales, Wadleigh himself is a lecturer and activist on sustainable development issues. Meanwhile, the festival's co-founder Michael Lang publishes his memoirs, *The Road to Woodstock*, in August [2009] and is planning a 40th anniversary concert in New York City in September. Socially, politically and musically, the legacy of Woodstock is all around us.

Lang, the festival's co-founder: "Obviously at the time Woodstock occurred we were in dire straits. We were in the middle of a horrible and unpopular war, with a very conservative and unresponsive government, and we of that generation were involved in lots of struggles for human rights. It was also the beginning of the green and organic movements. A lot of the seeds that have grown up today were planted then."

Wadleigh, the film's director: "In those days it was highly unusual to hold a festival on a farm. And that very simple stage, open to nature, was partly my idea. We wanted a kind of cathedral in the wilderness. When have you seen a concert in the past 20 years with no backdrop, no logos, no corporate sponsors? It was utter innocence."

Country Joe McDonald, performer: "I came early intending to watch as many acts as I could. I was surprised of course to see the size of the crowd, and they turned out to be another whole show in themselves."

Other Historic Events in 1969

April 24
US B-52 bombers launch the biggest attack yet on North Vietnam causing protests around the United States.

July 20
Apollo 11 lands on the moon. American Neil Armstrong is the first person to walk on its surface.

August 9–10
Pregnant actress Sharon Tate and four visiting friends are murdered in her rented home by acolytes of cult leader Charles Manson. The following night, members of the Manson "family" also murder Leno and Rosemary LaBianca.

October 29
The US Supreme Court orders school desegregation nationwide.

November 15
More than 500,000 protestors march in Washington, D.C., in the largest anti-war rally in US history.

November 24
Lieutenant William Calley is charged with the murder of 102 South Vietnamese civilians at My Lai.

December 1
The first US armed forces draft lottery since World War II is held in New York City.

December 24
A Rolling Stones concert at Altamont, California, erupts in violence and one spectator is killed.

Eddie Kramer, sound engineer: "Finding yourself in the middle of half a million people, just the physical magnitude of it was very impressive. I remember standing on the stage next to Bill Graham, the legendary promoter, who said to me: 'You know, Kramer, if these people decide to riot we're screwed.' But they never did, of course."

Wadleigh: "When all the fences came down, and it became clear they were going to lose millions of dollars, the organisers turned to me and said: 'You f---ing better do a good job, Wadleigh, or we're never going to get our money back. . . . '"

Melanie, performer: "When I went on that stage I was a complete unknown. But when I came off I was a celebrity. The next day they wanted me on television panel shows discussing the social significance of this event. I became the festival queen."

Carlos Santana, performer: "Woodstock was magical. We flew in by helicopter and backstage was like a disaster area. They told us we wouldn't go on until six or eight o'clock at night and we got there at eleven [A.M.]. I found Jerry Garcia and he had this great smile on his face and the next thing I know, I've taken something too. I thought by 8 P.M. I would come down and it wouldn't be a problem. Wrong!"

Organized Chaos

Wadleigh: "We had terrible problems with that storm. It nearly electrocuted a number of people, and destroyed several of our cameras. I've covered war zones, and it was not unlike that . . . except at least in Darfur you can get a little sleep. At Woodstock we had to stay awake for four days. That was helped by speed. The performers would not stop performing. Nobody wanted to get off the stage."

Kramer: "It was organised chaos. We were in the back, a couple of hundred feet behind the stage, in a tractor trailer, flying by the seat of our pants. We had no communication, no sight lines to the stage, no clue what was going on. Everything was up in the air."

David Dalton, former *Rolling Stone* writer: "One of the most terrifying things was the predominant sound of helicopters. When you're on acid, right in the middle of Vietnam, it was really bone-chilling. We thought they were going to start dropping napalm [a flammable chemical agent used during the Vietnam War]—and of course, we believed the Government was quite capable of that shit as well."

Wadleigh: "What we tried to do with the movie was something like *The Canterbury Tales*. We tried to make it not a Sixties movie but a timeless tale. So you have the policeman's tale, the tavern keeper's tale, the nude bather's tale, the toilet cleaner's tale. I think that's what makes it more than a rock movie, there's a sort of epic quality."

Dalton: "I enjoy watching it because, like any movie, it's a fantasy. It was created to maintain this whole illusion. Nowadays I don't think people go to festivals with that collective illusion that we're going to change the world."

Wadleigh: "[Glastonbury founder] Michael Eavis contacted me as soon as the film came out, and was highly influenced by it. And Glastonbury started the next year. I've been to several. I think you are very fortunate to have a festival with such integrity and vitality."

Kramer: "Ever since Woodstock I've avoided festivals like the plague. My son went to the second one and slept underneath a truck. It wasn't that great—but how could you possibly repeat Woodstock?"

Dalton: "The subsequent Woodstock festivals have been dreadful. I'm all in favour of people getting together in large groups, but the expectations were too high, too unrealistic and too pretentious."

Wadleigh: "There was little excuse for the other Woodstocks except to make a buck. They delivered none of the content, and the site they got was just very uncomfortable—big fences, like Guantánamo Bay [a detention facility at a US naval base in Cuba] or something. When you put on a festival like that how can you even call it Woodstock?"

Woodstock's Legacy

McDonald: "Woodstock's legacy is still a dream of a world of peace and love, and that is as alive today as back then. Almost everything today can be traced back to Woodstock in one way or another. I still feel like I am part of that counterculture generation."

Kramer: "I'm not a political person but you couldn't help but be swept up by that feeling: gosh, we can achieve anything."

> '[Woodstock] was a moment of hope and light in the middle of a dark period, and for us here in the US, the inauguration of [Barack] Obama was another one of those moments.'

Melanie: "People had a sense that we were going to change the world, for ever and for the better. And now they're sad that didn't happen, so there's a lot of cynicism. Maybe it was naive but that idealism was alive back then. I thought that was portrayed really beautifully in [the 1994 film] *Forrest Gump*, actually."

Lang: "It didn't take over America, but it wasn't that kind of revolution. It was more about the seeds that were planted. It was a moment of hope and light in the middle of a dark period, and for us here in the US, the inauguration of Obama was another one of those moments. Even *The Wall Street Journal* called it 'Washington's Woodstock.' I think there's a reason for that."

The Fans at Woodstock Were Outcasts Looking for Belonging

Joseph Sobran

In an editorial written twenty years after the event, a conservative columnist argues that Woodstock was not a cultural milestone. In fact, he maintains that personal and social devastation is the legacy of the era's free love and drug use. The festival was a gathering of freeloading loners looking for belonging, he claims, and the hippies who came to Woodstock claiming to reject the value system of their parents were not rebels. Indeed, he reasons that they were hungry for authority, all wearing the same bohemian uniform and speaking the same language. Unfortunately, he concludes, the belief that the type of people who attended Woodstock constitute a nation has led some to think that personal problems can be solved through political action. Joseph Sobran was an American journalist and a prominent conservative columnist.

SOURCE. Joseph Sobran, "A Nation of Loners," *National Review*, September 1, 1989. Reproduced by permission.

In early 1969 a quartet of young promoters decided to stage a weekend rock festival in Woodstock, New York, two hours from the Big Apple [New York City]. At first they figured on 25,000 fans. But as they lined up 27 acts for the August date, the projection grew. They were prepared—in food, sanitation, and medical facilities—for 150,000 people.

That turned out to be about a third of the total. Tickets were selling for $6 a head, but every hippie in the Northeast had heard about the big party, and by Friday, August 15, the roads to Woodstock were clogged with old Volkswagens crammed with scraggly-haired kids intent on three days of sex, drugs, and rock.

An Invasion of Unexpected Guests

The promoters had rented a field from a dairy farmer named Max Yasgur, and hoped to keep freeloaders out with makeshift fences. No use. The entire hippie economy was based on freeloading, and the minimal security arrangements couldn't cope with a half-million unexpected guests.

The townspeople had been nervous about the invasion. In fact, the festival wasn't allowed in Woodstock itself—it had had to be relocated to Bethel, fifty miles away. In those days upstate people were still afraid of hippies, especially in groups of 500,000 or so.

By Friday night the excitement was tremendous. None of the *really* big stars of rock—the Beatles, the Stones, Dylan—were there, but the roster was still impressive: Jimi Hendrix, Janis Joplin, Creedence Clearwater Revival, The Who, Johnny Winter, The Grateful Dead, Jefferson Airplane, Blood, Sweat, and Tears, Joan Baez, Arlo Guthrie, and such newcomers as Joe Cocker and Crosby, Stills, Nash, and Young. Later, having been at Woodstock would become a mark of status, for performers and fans alike. This was to be a legendary weekend.

"Hippies" stand in front of a teepee they built during the Woodstock festival. Conservative columnist Joseph Sobran argues that concertgoers were conformists, not rebels. (Getty Images.)

Hippie events tended to be—well, unstructured. To give you some idea of *how* unstructured Woodstock was, [social and political activist] Abbie Hoffman was partially responsible for security. Additional security was provided by a former standup comic named Wavy Gravy (née Hugh Romney), who ran a commune out west called the Hog Farm. A slight hitch developed when the Hog Farmers threatened to leave in protest against the killing of mosquitoes. The promoters had had the field sprayed with insecticide. For some hippies, insecticide was right next door to genocide.

Woodstock finally got under way, though not without a few more hitches. For one thing, it rained. Hard. Since shelter consisted almost exclusively of sleeping bags, this caught the crowd off guard. But they were having too much fun—ecstasy, really—to mind very much.

The rain didn't help the music, either. Acoustic conditions were already less than [classical pianist] Van Cliburn might have wished: loudspeakers, blaring into a pasture, rendering even Jimi Hendrix inaudible to much of the throng.

A Rejection of Traditional Values

The festival was attended by federal narcotics agents, who did make a hundred arrests for sale and possession of hard drugs, but made the strategic decision, lacking a half-million jail cells, to let pot-smoking ride. Marijuana enjoyed de facto legalization for the nonce. As for sex, there was plenty of it. In the general camaraderie, total strangers shared soggy sleeping bags. By day, some of them simply shared exposed patches of ground. Toplessness and nude bathing (in nearby ponds) were frequent.

It was all very Dionysian, a mass rejection of the false values of Ozzie and Harriet. From the bandstand, Country Joe McDonald led a joyous chant: "Give me an F! Give me a U!" until the crowd had spelled the *whole word*, bellowing it out in unison, not caring a whit if [President Richard] Nixon and [Vice President Spiro] Agnew and [FBI director] J. Edgar Hoover heard it all.

Leftist politics was taken for granted, but only as a sort of backdrop. When Abbie Hoffman tried to hog the microphone to deliver a political message while The Who was performing, Pete Townshend belted him from behind, decking him. Abbie scrambled off the bandstand and didn't come back.

Apart from that incident, all was peace and nonviolence. A gentle hippie oversoul seemed to suffuse the festival. As Wavy Gravy put it, years later, "The universe

> "Strangers had become brothers and sisters, smiling beatifically at each other with chemically induced inner peace."

took over and did a little dance. . . . And you could just feel these little tendrils of invisible energies kind of like—I felt at times like a marionette almost." Strangers had become brothers and sisters, smiling beatifically at each other with chemically induced inner peace.

But by Saturday afternoon, there were more hitches. The field was sheer mud. Food had just about run out. So had toilet paper. The Port-O-Sans smelled so foul that people were using the earth itself, and it was getting . . . noticeable. One youth was run over in his sleeping bag by a tractor hauling away Port-O-San deposits; he died.

At one point there was a serious scare. Several helicopters were approaching ominously. Was Nixon launching an aerial assault? No. It turned out that the U.S. Army and National Guard were flying food and medical supplies to Woodstock Nation. On Sunday morning more food—eggs, doughnuts, cereal, milk, sandwiches—arrived, courtesy of local residents. Woodstock Nation had quickly become reliant on the adult world it had tried to do without for the weekend. About the only thing there was no shortage of was drugs.

Max Yasgur's farm, green on Friday, was a brown expanse of mud, garbage, and hippie dung when everyone left Monday morning. The odor lingered strongly for nearly a year. Even after that, for two more years, you could still smell it every time the weather was hot—the after-birth of a nation.

Questioning the Glory of Woodstock

Woodstock is a legend now. If you weren't there, you are given to understand, you really missed something—an unrepeatable instant of hope and joy and brotherhood, and an epiphany of a better world that might be. "It

The Iconic Woodstock Poster

The 1969 Woodstock poster—a dove perched on the neck of a guitar—has become an iconic image that for many reflects the values of the counterculture movement of the 1960s, and perhaps of a generation. However, it was not the first design for the event. David Byrd created the original poster for the festival to be held in Wallkill, New York. Byrd's poster contained an image of Aquarius, a sign of the zodiac meant to symbolize the Aquarian Age of equality, peace, and harmony. When Wallkill officials banned the festival at the last minute, the promoters commissioned graphic artist Arnold Skolnick to create a new poster. According to Skolnick, catbirds that he had been sketching inspired the bird's design. Originally, the famed "catbird" dove was perched on a flute because he was listening to jazz. The final product was a poster with a red background, a blue and green guitar, and a white dove. A unique feature of the poster was that no artists were given top billing: The names of artists appearing were printed in the same type size and in alphabetical order. Promoter Michael Lang's vision was that the concert would be about countercultural values, not the performers themselves.

The conflicting stories of the poster's origins also reflects the mythic nature of Woodstock. Skolnick contests promoter Michael Lang's claim that the idea for the dove on the guitar was Lang's. According to Skolnick, until the poster was completed, Lang had never seen it. Skolnick claims never to have spoken to Lang. He also disputes stories that he was inspired by his sons and a nonexistent daughter. Nevertheless, conflicting stories about the poster continue to be told in books, articles, and on websites. Despite the poster's mythology, Skolnick maintains that he was simply a graphic artist providing a design solution that happened to become famous.

confirmed my sense that class, race, and gender divisions could be transcended," one participant is quoted as saying in *Life*'s twentieth-anniversary commemoration of the magic weekend. Many others speak in the same tones. There has been talk of recreating the moment, but the idea has been tied up in legal wrangles over promotional rights.

Pundits can't seem to resist talking about Woodstock in grandiose terms. Shortly after the event, *Time* spoke of it as auguring a new value system that could change (for the better, of course) the American national character. Today, it is generally lauded as a milestone of the counterculture.

Which it was, in a way. *Life*'s delirious quotations from celebrants are more than balanced by others who speak of the drug abuse, their own subsequent problems with drugs, the friends who later died from overdoses. Several of the rockers who performed at Woodstock have also died, most of them from drug excesses. Abbie Hoffman, who resurfaced after ten years on the lam for a cocaine rap, killed himself in April [1989], using sleeping pills.

Another glory of Woodstock, free love, has also come a cropper in the years since. Like drugs, it has been a source of personal and social devastation over time. The cult of the ecstatic moment looks much less promising than it did in 1969. The destruction has been worst in the chief target of liberal solicitude, the black inner cities. Dionysus has worn out his welcome.

Even so, nostalgic books and articles on Woodstock flood us. Most of them suggest that the weekend utopia in the mud stands as a model for emulation.

But despite the grand terms in which Woodstock is praised (and sometimes denounced), one of the laudatory books, Jack Curry's *Woodstock: The Summer of Our Lives*, inadvertently touches on what may be the real meaning of the event: "This had been a convention of 500,000 people who had always thought they were freaks, alone."

Janis Joplin said something like that to the crowd from the Woodstock bandstand: "We used to think of ourselves as little clumps of weirdos. But now we're a whole new minority group." A year later she was dead, of a drug overdose. (She was also alcoholic.)

Life quotes another Woodstockian: "I flung myself into the counterculture without looking back. It seemed like the outcasts had found acceptance. I had friends for the first time."

Hungry for Authority

Woodstock enabled such people, multiplied by a few hundred thousand, to think they were the wave of the future, their leaning on each other an event of world-historical importance. But to read Curry's book is to find, between the lines of congratulation, a series of sad case histories of kids who had always felt like losers, until the big party. And afterward. There is the pathos of self-delusion in the way they profess to have drawn sustaining—almost salvific [redemptive]—inspiration from an inordinately publicized rock concert.

Woodstock's mythic status as a peak spiritual, cultural, or political moment is belied by the way these poor kids couldn't even manage a mildly rebellious weekend without succor from grownups. In a way, one could wish it had at least been a case of flaming youth burning off animal energies. It was so much less than that. Even its devil-may-care image is too flattering.

> The hippies . . . were positively hungry for authority. They settled for the only form they could get, which was peer pressure.

Doesn't anyone remember the Sixties? The hippies weren't rebels. They were positively hungry for authority. They settled for the only form they could get, which was peer pressure. Their "rebellion" was all fashion and imitation, mass-market bohemianism. The long hair, love beads, and tie-dyed jeans were the nearest approximation to a uniform they could achieve, They all talked alike, in a studied slang that adults, on casual contact, found refreshing and exotic. It got dull very quickly. The stereotypes were true because hippies mimicked each other. They were usually lonely and unloved kids who felt they had to be each other's role models. They were wrongly suspected of wanting to destroy society when they were only destroying themselves. As at Woodstock.

Loners have a way of finding each other. What Woodstock proves is that when their numbers reach critical mass, they become a market, and you can herd them together and tell them things they desperately want to hear from somebody: that they're winners, that they constitute a nation, that they hold the hope of the world, and that all their unresolved personal problems are really only one big political problem that can be solved instantaneously. Some of them will go on believing it for twenty years.

Some Festivalgoers Continue to Promote the Ideals of the Woodstock Generation

Paul Lieberman

In the viewpoint that follows, a reporter writes that he and his fellow Woodstock pilgrims continue to be social activists. He explains that he and his Woodstock traveling companions were at the time serving their community in President Lyndon Johnson's anti-poverty program. He admits that their primary goal was to go to Woodstock for the music and that they rationalized the purchase of their bus using government funds—it was to be a roving tutorial center to reach children outside Massachusetts mill towns. The bus did serve some good as his friends served pancakes for hungry festivalgoers passing by, he asserts. In his view, his story is

SOURCE. Paul Lieberman, "Frankly Dankly, the Bus of '69; An Oil-dripping Heap Painted with the Name of a Fictitious Band Took Young Activists to Woodstock, and Their Own Turning Points," *Los Angeles Times*, August 15, 2009, p. A1. Reproduced by permission.

more than mere nostalgia, because he and his fellow Woodstock pilgrims continue to effect change. Paul Lieberman is an investigative journalist and a staff writer for the *Los Angeles Times*.

The statute of limitations should protect us from prosecution, so let the truth be told—we used anti-poverty funds to buy the Frankly Dankly bus in the landmark summer of '69. One of our group still insists we "passed the hat" to pay for the thing. But he's a respectable lawyer now, so we'll allow him that fog of memory. Everyone else is willing to 'fess up that we dipped into money intended to help the poor to procure the oil-leaking school bus we saw sitting in a lot with a "For Sale" sign.

Soldiers in the War on Poverty

Oh, we had a cover story for spending the $500—that we could use a roving tutorial center to reach kids beyond the old mill towns where we were soldiers in the war on poverty. We no doubt hoped that would be the fate of the bus, eventually. But first we tore out the seats, painted the sides bright red, white and blue, and etched on the name of a nonexistent rock band, Frankly Dankly and His Seven Little All-Americans. Then we loaded it up with turkeys and pancake mix and headed over the Berkshires to a muddy farmland in Bethel, N.Y.

We actually had tickets for the three-day Woodstock Music and Art Fair, our coterie of idealistic college students who exemplified an era that blurred the line between political activism and experimenting with new lifestyles. We'd spend days helping low-income families find housing, then gather at night to mull over our motives and shed our inhibitions with encounter

> The Frankly Dankly saga is not just another baby boomer [Woodstock] nostalgia trip, for from our crew came a movement that's a lightning-rod today.

groups that left us half-naked on the floor. We would open a community center with a parade down Main Street.

This weekend's 40th anniversary of Woodstock is spawning a new torrent of recollections of that summer that may leave generations born before and after screaming, "Enough!" But trust me, the Frankly Dankly saga is not just another baby boomer nostalgia trip, for from our crew came a movement that's a lightning-rod today.

Frustrated Social Activists

The Office of Economic Opportunity had been established by President Lyndon Johnson to spearhead his Great Society anti-poverty efforts, but President [Richard] Nixon was skeptical of it and in 1969 put a pair of up-and-coming Republicans in charge. Let's not blame Donald Rumsfeld and Dick Cheney, however, for what we did with their money—North Adams, Mass. was far below their radar.

Our adventure began with two fellow Williams College students who had spent time in this community of 18,000 built around a brick factory that once made Civil War uniforms. The southward flight of the textile industry had devastated New England, so a team of 18 was assembled to help out here and in nearby Adams, some with full slots in VISTA (the Volunteers in Service to America), others dubbed VISTA summer associates.

Several of the group had just graduated from college, but two girls from Bennington College were merely through freshman year, and sauntered about in big, floppy hats. I was only a year older but had street cred as a New Yorker who'd marched in my first demonstration while in my mother's womb, though I'd also worked as a riflery instructor, trained by the NRA [National Rifle Association].

Bill Cummings was the son of a West Point graduate and had married a fellow military brat, Salli Benedict.

Bill had become disenchanted with the war after seeing the wounded in a hospital in the Philippines, where his father was based while staging night bombing raids over Vietnam. Chris Kinnell was a lanky basketball player from supposedly laid back Pacific Palisades. Bruce Plenk was a self-described "save the world type" from Utah who believed that a crusade for social change could be waged with "a lightness and fun to it."

Wade Rathke was not about lightness and fun. The onetime Eagle Scout from New Orleans was, like Cummings, married already at 20. Though he attended the same elite college as us, Wade had supported himself for a time driving a forklift. He had taken a year off to do draft counseling only to become disillusioned when better-off kids were all that came through the door. Now he'd lean silently against a wall at our meetings, a cigarette dangling from his mouth.

Our orientation coincided with a Boston rally of the National Welfare Rights Organization, where we met Saul Alinsky, who had become a legend organizing around the Chicago stockyards. "When you come into a community, you don't have 'issues,'" Alinsky told us. "You have 'sad scenes.' Your job is to turn those sad scenes into issues."

But how many college kids had what it took to go door-to-door in housing projects to persuade welfare mothers to sit in at a government office to obtain back-to-school clothing for their kids? The Welfare Rights honchos saw one candidate in our crowd, Rathke. I think many of us were relieved when he agreed to organize the city of Springfield, an hour southeast of our western Massachusetts towns.

For the rest of us, the work seemed snake-bitten that summer. We spent weeks promoting a meeting of tenants at a church in North Adams only to have astronaut Neil Armstrong pick that night to step on the moon. The two locals who showed up must have been the

Wade Rathke, one of the young activists who bought a bus using government funds to attend Woodstock, went on to found ACORN, a collection of community-based social reform organizations. (**Associated Press.**)

only ones without TVs. It poured the day we opened the community center in an old supermarket. Still, we danced into the wee hours to a band that did perfect covers of Three Dog Night hits ("One is the loneliest number . . . ") and soon would play as a warm-up act at . . . well, enter the bus.

Wavy Gravy: Saint Misbehavin'

Wavy Gravy . . . is more active—and more effective—in the world than he was 27 years ago when, still known as Hugh Romney, he stood on the Woodstock stage and announced, "What we have in mind is breakfast in bed for 400,000!" He was at Woodstock as a member of an entertainment/activist commune known as the Hog Farm. Today, the Hog Farm [headquartered in Berkeley, California] still exists. . . . But Mr. Gravy . . . has expanded his activities over the past two-and-a-half decades to include codirectorship (with his wife, Jahanara) of Camp Winnarainbow, a performing arts program for children which takes over the Hog Farm for 10 weeks every summer, and the organization of all-star rock concerts to raise money for a variety of environmental, progressive, political, and charitable causes, most notably Seva, a foundation he cofounded 18 years ago, initially to combat preventable and curable blindness in the Third World.

He may be best known to millions as a cosmic cut-up and the inspiration for a Ben & Jerry's ice cream flavor—"I am an activist clown and frozen dessert," he says—but it is because of his good work on behalf of the planet and its least fortunate residents that Wavy Gravy has achieved his own brand of sainthood. . . . Wavy says, "Some people tell me I'm a saint, I tell them I'm Saint Misbehavin'."

SOURCE. *Derk Richardson, "A Clown for Our Time,"* Yoga Journal, *March/April 1997.*

Admitting the Real Motive for the Trip

Ads for the Aug. 15–17 Woodstock festival promised "Three Days of Peace & Music," peace first, music second. The promoters expected 50,000 people for a celebration of an egalitarian spirit with "painting and sculpture on trees [by] accomplished artists, ghetto artists and would-be artists." But what attracted us were acts such as Janis Joplin, Jimi Hendrix and Crosby, Stills, Nash & Young. If purchased well in advance, three-day tickets cost $18, so the Bennington girls collected that and mailed in our money. Cummings floated the idea of buying the school bus a week into August, saying we could reach rural families. That's when I piped up, "Why kid ourselves?" We all knew the real motive. Counterarguments flew back: The bus cost next to nothing. We were paying ourselves a pittance, $25 a week. We could say the $500 was from donations from college alumni, never mind that all our funds were mingled. But I was an effective spoilsport. We voted down the purchase.

Then everyone got drunk, or whatever, and in the morning we bought the bus.

We did paint it off-hours. Then we paid a local sign man to letter on "Frankly Dankly and his Seven Little All-Americans," a name fellow students used for a phantom band they kept promising would play at parties. We bought sleeveless T-shirts and painted "F.D." in red on each. Salli, our Earth mother at 21, roasted the turkeys. We took off mid-morning Friday, Aug. 15, our kazoos playing Canned Heat's "Going Up the Country."

The bus drew stares whenever we stopped, which was at almost every gas station because it wouldn't hold oil—there was a reason we got it for $500. In quaint Millbrook, N.Y., a couple hurried their children into their car at the sight of our bus. There was a power to the budding Youth Culture, even if it split our society.

A Blur of Memories

The traffic became inch-along dense miles from Max Yasgur's farm, where the festival would be, but we talked our way through one checkpoint by insisting, "We've got Mr. Dankly's equipment in the back!" Then a second security guy checked, saw only our kazoos, and guided us into a field with two dozen other painted buses. Mud caked the sneakers and moccasins of the thousands of youths in their own floppy hats and painted t-shirts trudging like refugees in a war zone past where cattle had grazed a day before.

We joined the procession and 45 minutes later heard the dim sound of music. We glimpsed the makeshift towers behind the stage. They'd given up on taking tickets. We were directed up the far side of a hill, sensing the mass of people but seeing little.

Finally, we made a left and took in the spectacle through dimming light: We were halfway up a natural amphitheater that once was an alfalfa field but now resembled a staging ground for the Roman legions. Though we were a quarter mile from the stage, it looked as if every inch was packed, with more people than we'd seen in one place.

Years later, we could not be sure what we witnessed and what we saw in the Woodstock movie. A few of us thought we caught the opening act, Richie Havens, but the first I recall was Country Joe McDonald, doing his anti-war ditty: "And it's one, two, three / What are we fighting for? / Don't ask me, I don't give a damn / Next stop is Vietnam."

Then I went exploring up the hill and lost our group. The youth culture that had gotten us so much attention en route swallowed me up. After the night ended with Joan Baez singing "We Shall Overcome," I feared I'd never find the bus, but did, somehow. The next morning, Bill and Salli made pancakes for hundreds of passersby. So the bus did do some good for humanity.

> [Festivalgoer] Bill Cummings is a PhD ecologist who monitors development projects in Pakistan.

Saturday was a wet blur. Someone had to wake Bill so he could hear Sly and the Family Stone. Sunday, we were gone long before Hendrix performed his agonized Star Spangled Banner. We were intent on being at our $25-a-week jobs Monday morning.

Before we knew it, most of us were back at college, but a core stayed in North Adams and engineered one tangible success, construction of low-cost housing. Little was said of the bus, which never made any community rounds. Suffering from a cracked block, it was last spotted in a field, left to rust into oblivion with our memories.

Still Addressing Social Issues

It took work to find some of the crew: Bill Cummings is a PhD ecologist who monitors development projects in Pakistan but lives outside Chapel Hill, N.C. Though he's no longer married to Salli, she's there too, directing public health programs, the

> [Festivalgoer Salli Cummings is] directing public health programs, the latest targeting obesity among poor women.

latest targeting obesity among poor women. They dote on four grandkids and recently took a couple to an outdoor concert by Bob Dylan, Willie Nelson and John Mellencamp.

After years as a legal aid attorney, Bruce Plenk coordinates solar energy projects for the city of Tucson. Our basketball player from Pali high, Chris Kinnell, is a minister in upstate New York, just back from a mission to Zimbabwe. The guy who swore we passed the hat to buy the bus, John Kitchen, is a lawyer who works with the disabled in New Hampshire. One of the Bennington girls became a psychologist.

Wade Rathke, in contrast, was a snap to find. He's been living what he calls his "Britney Spears moment" since the presidential race that put Barack Obama, a one-time community organizer, in the White House. That's when the organization Wade founded, ACORN, hired 8,000 canvassers to register 1.3 million voters. Backers of Sen. John McCain accused it of trying to steal the election.

Wade never did return to school that fall of '69, but the local papers reported his progress in Springfield, where he led hundreds of welfare mothers demanding vouchers for winter coats. He was thinking of returning south to establish "a strong conflict group," concentrating on poor whites. Then he was gone, to Arkansas, to launch the Assn. of Community Organizations for Reform Now.

Nowadays, he's a favorite villain of the right. "I'm not surprised that I'm seen as a dangerous dude," Wade said when we reconnected for the first time in four decades. "In fact, I am."

I asked him about his bid to organize "the rest of the planet," as one report put it, but I mostly wanted his explanation for missing the Frankly Dankly bus. "Knew about the bus," he replied. "We had seats on the bus."

It seems his wife, Lee, (now his ex) had been intent on going with us and shelled out $36 for two sets of tickets, but Wade was not going to be diverted from his Welfare Rights work. Yet over the years his memory combined the summer's events into a semi-fable that had Woodstock weekend as the turning point in his life. The tale had him driving his Ford Econoline van to meet us only to have it break down, so he hitched instead to Springfield and resolved to become an organizer.

> The summer of '69 was a turning point for me. . . . I gravitated to investigative reporting, and projects on working conditions and healthcare.

"Who knows where I would have wound up if I had gotten on the bus with you guys," he said. "I might have thought I had a future shaking a tambourine in a rock 'n' roll band."

The summer of '69 was a turning point for me, as well. I found I was a pretty good observer and, perhaps, had a conscience. Later, when I gravitated to investigative reporting, and projects on working conditions and healthcare, I thought of Saul Alinsky's exhortation to turn "sad scenes" into issues. But I was pulled toward entertaining people, as well, and thought of our embrace of lightness, a quality often overwhelmed by the meanness of today.

My wife and I go to the Berkshires each summer, and North Adams is a regular stop, for the factory that made Civil War uniforms has become a great museum, MASS MoCA [Massachusetts Museum of Contemporary Art]. I take back roads, indulging the fantasy that I'll spot kids playing in a patch of high grass, in the corroded hull of vehicle with a trace of odd lettering on its side.

The Woodstock Festival Is Now More Myth than Reality

Jacob Bernstein

Photo on following page: The front page of the *New York Daily News* on August 17, 1969, failed to account fully for the importance of Woodstock. (**NY Daily News via Getty Images.**)

The following viewpoint argues that Woodstock's enduring mythology is a result of the media's failure to foresee the enormity of the event. The author claims that neither the *New York Times* nor *Rolling Stone* considered Woodstock newsworthy at the time. The front-page story in the *Times* came from freelancer Barnard Collier, who paid his own way to attend the festival, and the famed photos in *Life* magazine came from a nineteen-year-old intern, Lawrence Kramer, who had never had a photo assignment before. The fact that the media regret their failure to anticipate the enormity of gathering so many young people tougher for the biggest concert ever has led to their making more of Woodstock than it was, Bernstein reasons, thus trivializing what young people have endured since then. Jacob Bernstein is a regular contributor to *Women's Wear Daily*.

SOURCE. Jacob Bernstein, "The Making of the Woodstock Myth," *Women's Wear Daily*, vol. 193, August 11, 2009, p. 8. Reproduced by permission.

SUNDAY NEWS
NEW YORK'S PICTURE NEWSPAPER ®

FiNAL ★★★★   **20¢**

Vol. 49. No. 16   Copr. 1969 News Syndicate Co. Inc.   New York, N.Y. 10017, Sunday, August 17, 1969*   WEATHER: Cloudy, warm and humid.

HIPPIES MIRED IN SEA OF MUD

NEWS photo by Paul DeMaria

They Don't Melt... Rocksters, undaunted by rain, mud and food shortages, trek to Woodstock folk-rock festival at White Lake, N.Y. Several thousand fled the desolated area and headed for Manhattan in a fleet of buses last night and this morning. The exodus made little dent in the crowd, numbering more than 400,000. —*Stories p. 3; other pics centerfold*

Some historical events are palpably momentous from the second they occur. Pearl Harbor. The fall of the Berlin wall. The first time man walked on the moon.

The Woodstock Music and Art Fair, which celebrates its 40th anniversary this weekend [August 2009], wasn't one of them.

A Lack of Media Interest

Jann Wenner, owner and editor of *Rolling Stone*, the preeminent music publication of the age, didn't even go.

"Who wants to come to New York in August?" he says of the festival, which took place at Max Yasgur's 600-acre dairy farm in the Bethel area of the Catskills from Aug. 15 to 17, 1969. "I lived on the West Coast then. I'd seen Jimi Hendrix three or four times already. I'd seen more than enough of the Grateful Dead."

> 'At the time, no one really knew [Woodstock] was going to be a story.'

The *New York Times* was barely paying attention to the concert and got its big front-page wrap-up from a reporter named Barnard Collier, who went there on his own dime, called his editors at the paper and recalls saying something along the lines of, "You're making a big mistake not devoting more resources to this." (As he remembers it, they hastily sent up a couple of other staffers on the second day, when the crowds were simply too big to ignore.)

Nor did the Associated Press predict the party of the century, which is why many of the images it syndicated to publications like *Life* magazine came from a 19-year-old intern named Lawrence Kramer, who'd never had a photo assignment before and presumably got the job because no one else wanted to go. "You're a little spoiled if Woodstock is your first assignment," says Kramer (now a digital media consultant). "But at the time, no one really knew it was going to be a story."

Even after Janis Joplin; Crosby, Stills, Nash & Young; Arlo Guthrie; Jefferson Airplane, and Carlos Santana finished their sets, few in the mainstream media (as it's now called) heralded the weekend in Upstate New York as the most important rock 'n' roll event of all time (or the signature cultural event of the Sixties).

An Epic Mess

Partly this is because Woodstock was, logistically speaking, a total disaster. Nearly 200,000 tickets were sold, and between 400,000 and 500,000 people showed up, according to *Time* magazine. The traffic jam leading up to the fairground was described by *Rolling Stone*'s man on the ground, Greil Marcus, as an epic mess comparable to the famous scene in Jean-Luc Godard's New Wave film "Weekend."

Then came the rain, the mud, the food and water shortages and the "brown acid" circulating throughout the crowd, which sent many to the makeshift infirmary. "It was hot and uncomfortable; there was no sanitation; people were sick; it was really bad," Marcus remembers.

Of course, few people now remember Woodstock as the world's worst traffic jam, a standoff in which the 346 police officers walked off the job just before the festival's scheduled start, or a concert at which helicopters flew overhead, dropping fresh clothes into the wet crowd. It's become something larger, vaguer and more symbolic—a kaleidoscopic fashion show for the Sixties characterized by groovy music, peace signs, fabulous clothes and endless free drugs. But at the time, the indignities people suffered at the festival dominated headlines and overshadowed the tremendous accomplishment of gathering all those kids in one place for the biggest concert ever.

"400,000 Jam Rock Festival in the Catskills" read the headline for the *Washington Post*'s first front-page story on the affair. That article didn't even mention the bands playing the festival until nearly a thousand words had

Memorable Woodstock Remarks

- Designed to minimize wait times between acts, designers developed a revolving stage. However, the plan did not take into account performers who stood on the sidelines to watch. One crewman remarked, "Grace Slick and Janis Joplin and every-body were standing on it and you can't just sweep them off with a broom."

- During the torrential rains that descended on the festival, some feared that artists would be electro-cuted. Being warned of the risk, Alvin Lee of Ten Years After responded, "Oh, come on; if I get elec-trocuted at Woodstock, we'll sell lots of records."

- The *New York Post* rock critic said that the per-formance of "The Star-Spangled Banner" by Jimi Hendrix at the close of Woodstock was "the single greatest moment of the Sixties." However, few wit-nessed the live performance: most concert goers had left by the time Hendrix came on stage early Monday morning.

SOURCE. *Spencer Bright, "Forty Far-Out Facts You Never Knew About Woodstock,"* Daily Mail *(UK), August 8, 2009.*

been devoted to car troubles, sick attendees and the boy who died when he fell asleep in a sleeping bag on a farm nearby and got run over by a tractor (one of only two people who died out of close to half a million).

The *New York Times* was vicious. An Op-Ed was titled "Nightmare in the Catskills" and went as follows: "The dreams of marijuana and rock music that drew 300,000 fans and hippies to the Catskills had little more sanity than the impulses that drive the lemmings to the sea. They ended in a nightmare of mud and stagnation. . . . What kind of culture is it that can produce so colossal a mess?"

Hearing this today absolutely tickles Collier. "Someone should suggest that [comedian and TV show host] Stephen Colbert read it on air on Woodstock's anniversary. What it looked like to me was a rare example of nonviolent anarchy, but newspapers are terrified of anarchy."

Still, if much of the initial post-Woodstock press coverage was negative, it didn't take long for the media to pivot from covering it as a domestic disturbance to dubbing it "history's biggest happening," per *Time* magazine only a week after the event.

And that troubles some members of the Woodstock press corps, who admit to being a little perplexed and exhausted by the festival's enduring mythology. It's like having failed to properly anticipate just how momentous Woodstock would be, the media has now spent an eternity kicking itself and telling people, "It'll never be like that again."

> Some members of the Woodstock press corps . . . admit to being a little perplexed and exhausted by the festival's enduring mythology.

"My generation has worked really hard to insist that its history was privileged in a special way," Marcus says. "We lived in what we considered to be the most glorious of all times and have devoted the rest of our lives to making sure no one ever forgets that. The result is to trivialize everything younger people have lived through, and part of the reason we've been able to do that is that every time this history is sold back to them, people line up to buy it. It's tremendously destructive and sad."

Wade Lawrence, director of The Museum at Bethel Woods, agrees journalists are laying it on a little thick as the 40th anniversary approaches, but isn't sure that's anything remarkable. "Woodstock has been overmythologized and pumped up, but I'm not sure there's anything wrong with that. It means something to an awful lot of fifty-something and sixty-something people who were there and it changed their lives in a lot of ways. So was it pumped up? Yeah. But name a world event that doesn't get pumped up by the media."

Woodstock Was More Complex than the Myth to Which It Has Been Reduced

Maurice Isserman

In the following viewpoint, a festival attendee compares the gathering of Woodstock veterans to American Civil War commemorative events that reconcile divisions between North and South. For him, visiting the Woodstock museum at Bethel Woods, the original concert site, was not about what divided the United States back then, but the values that unite Americans today. The Woodstock mythology—that it was a time of innocence that stands apart from the darker moments of the 1960s—is inaccurate and unfair, in the author's view. Although Woodstock was not a demonstration, it was a reflection of the generational upheaval of the 1960s. The discord created by the civil-rights and anti-Vietnam War movements set the stage for Woodstock. Indeed, he argues, Woodstock

SOURCE. Maurice Isserman, "3 Days of Peace and Music, 40 Years of Memory," *Chronicle of Higher Education*, vol. 55, August 10, 2009. Copyright 2009 Maurice Isserman. Reproduced by permission of the author.

veterans inspired by the festival would participate in the massive national demonstrations against the Vietnam War later in 1969. Maurice Isserman is a history professor and the author of *America Divided: The Civil War of the 1960s.*

In describing the 1913 reunion of Union and Confederate veterans at Gettysburg, the historian David Blight noted that "the veterans were men out of another time, icons that stimulated a sense of pride, history, and amusement all at once." To Americans of a younger generation who attended or read about the commemorative events, the veterans "were at once the embodiment of Civil War nostalgia, symbols of a lost age of heroism, and the fulfillment of that most human of needs—civic and spiritual reconciliation."

A Woodstock Veteran

Without wishing to stretch the analogy too far, I felt a little like one of those ancient Civil War veterans this summer, when I found myself taking my 14-year-old son, David, to the Museum at Bethel Woods, site of the original Woodstock music festival. It was my first time there since August 1969. Our national military parks are littered with monuments marking the exact spot where this or that regiment took its heroic stand, or this or that general fell while leading his men to glory. For my part, I tried to pick out and show David the exact spot where I stood in the crowd while singing along with Country Joe McDonald's "I-Feel-Like-I'm-Fixin'-to-Die Rag." David was impressed (and also, I suspect, amused).

Anyway, thanks to Woodstock, the dairy farmer Max Yasgur's 600 acres, including the natural amphitheater formed by its sloping fields and overlooking the lake at its base, remain as pristinely pastoral as they were 40 years ago. Like our more famous Civil War battlefields, they have been spared the shopping malls and

Exhibits at the Bethel Woods Center for the Arts memorialize the Woodstock festival and attract those nostalgic about the event. (AFP/Getty Images.)

tract housing that might otherwise have befallen them. Minus the stage, and the half-million or so festivalgoers, the field still powerfully evokes those much-celebrated "Three Days of Peace and Music." . . .

There were only a few people on the grounds at Bethel, N.Y., when David and I visited, but I'm sure that with the anniversary, both the museum and the site will be crowded with nostalgic visitors, including my fellow veterans, as well as many pilgrims born in the years since 1969. What will they be seeking?

Blight has argued that the purpose and spirit of Civil War commemorations underwent a significant shift in the decades following the 1860s. At first such gatherings served as a reminder of the issues and passions that had driven North and South into their conflict. But by the time veterans of the Blue and Gray met at Gettysburg, 50 years later, the anniversaries had come instead to symbolize the end of sectional division and the eclipse of the issues (including, unfortunately, any national commitment to black equality) that had loomed large during the war and in its immediate aftermath. Woodstock nostalgia and commemorations, on the contrary, have tended to be about reconciliation, with an emphasis on the values that unite Americans across generational and partisan lines. Woodstock's enduring mythic legacy—a dream of innocence, redemption, self-reliance, and self-invention that owes so much to the traditional American narrative—began to define the event in popular and historical memory even before Jimi Hendrix brought the concert to an end on Monday morning, August 18, 1969, with his inspired retooling of the national anthem.

Dire Predictions

In the months leading up to Woodstock, however, many observers had predicted the festival would prove a disaster. After all, the protests at the Democratic National Convention in Chicago just a year earlier had also been billed as a kind of countercultural festival, and they had turned (largely because of the heavy-handedness of Chicago authorities, it should be said) into a weeklong street battle between demonstrators and Mayor Richard J. Daley's police. Only some 10,000 or so had been involved in that donnybrook [a wild fight; brawl], but 100,000 or more were expected to show up for Woodstock—a very scary prospect to many people, especially older residents of upstate New York. In his memoir, [festival coproducer Michael] Lang recalls the opposition from local people in Wallkill, the town where Woodstock was originally intended to be held. "The phone line at our field office was getting bombarded with death threats from hippie-hating residents," he writes. And the callers weren't kidding: A blast of shotgun pellets ripped into the festival's office walls one dark night. A barrage of legal challenges finally forced the organizers to look elsewhere for a concert site, which is how they wound up in Bethel, with less than a month to get everything prepared.

The organizers held on to their original vision in the face of the hostility—the opposition crucial to the mythic underpinnings of the event, for an epic requires adversity. The fact that the organizers were making it up as they went along only added to the appeal. Improvisation and serendipity were the keys to Woodstock's success.

Once the festival began, everyone involved persevered in the face of the astonishing unexpected crush of humanity that showed up. The scale of the event, while the source of so many of its logistical difficulties, also made the problems seem like petty annoyances easy to overlook. From the moment I crested the hill above the stage and looked down on the multitudes gathered below, I had a sense of having unexpectedly blundered into the opportunity to Make History—a bracing feeling that I've seldom felt thereafter, and one that went a long way to compensate for the fact that during the next 24 hours I spent perched on a soggy blanket on a muddy hillside, I would neither eat nor sleep.

The View from the Perimeters

From the adult perimeters, the situation looked dire. Parents, alerted to troubling developments by news reports (the New York State Thruway shut down, food supplies proving inadequate, and so on) naturally worried about their children's well-being; mine certainly did. Gov. Nelson Rockefeller declared Bethel a disaster area on the festival's second day. He wanted to send in the National

Guard to begin evacuating the site; the festival organizers persuaded him to send medical teams and food instead. According to Barnard L. Collier, the *New York Times* reporter assigned to cover the event, he was pressured by his editors (including the executive editor, James Reston, who seemed to harbor a sharp animus against youth culture and protest in general) to report that Woodstock was "a social catastrophe in the making." But, to Collier's credit, his story "300,000 at Folk-Rock Fair Camp Out in a Sea of Mud," running on the front page of that weekend's Sunday newspaper, quoted Lang's reassuring description of the gathering as "the quietest, most well-behaved 300,000 people in one place that can be imagined." More significant (since Lang's objectivity could be questioned), Collier also quoted an unnamed state-police official who described himself as "dumbfounded" by both the size and the good nature of the crowd.

The *Times* bigwigs, at odds with their reporters on the scene, clung to their grumpy naysaying a little longer; that Monday they ran an editorial titled "Nightmare in the Catskills." But the very next day, in a dramatic reversal, they wrote another editorial, titled "Morning After at Bethel," deciding that Woodstock had, after all, been "essentially a phenomenon of innocence." Perhaps the editors finally realized that a good percentage of their future subscription base had camped out on Yasgur's farm that weekend. The conclusion of the editorial anticipated, with a certain tongue-in-cheek appreciation, the possibility of future reunions of Woodstock veterans: "For comrades-in-rock, like comrades-in-arms, need great days to remember and embroider. With Henry the Fifth they could say at Bethel, 'He that outlives this day, and comes safe home, will stand a-tiptoe when this day is nam'd.'"

> The quintessential '60s' event . . . [Woodstock] was also thought to stand apart from the decade's darker impulses.

Inaccurate Clichés and Unfair Dichotomies

Woodstock would go down in history as a moment of reconciliation rather than confrontation largely because, in the end, nobody wound up beating up or shooting or cursing at anyone else. Police officers, hippies, and Bethel's residents were on their best behavior, and a great sigh of relief was heard across the news-media landscape. So Woodstock became, on the one hand, the quintessential "60s" event, the culmination of a decade of challenge and change, but was also thought to stand apart from the decade's darker impulses, as a moment of restored innocence and good feeling in a time of turmoil and discord. [Director Michael] Wadleigh's documentary, *Woodstock*, opens with a view of Yasgur's fields in the days leading up to the festival, with two hippie guys riding by on horseback, their blond, flower-child girlfriends clinging behind, while Crosby, Stills and Nash can be heard on the soundtrack singing, "It's been a long time coming." Cut to the cows. Cut to the tractors. Cut to the Woodstock stage under construction. Welcome to the American Eden. . . .

> Woodstock was not a protest, and many of those attending never had attended, and never would, a political demonstration.

And with Altamont,[1] of course, the countercultural Eden would be down for the count.

But the Woodstock-Altamont antithesis isn't very satisfactory. The kids who showed up at the latter could not have been very different from those of us who went to Woodstock. A bad choice of venue (racetrack rather than farmland) and a worse choice of security (Hell's Angels rather than the Hog Farm commune) made the difference.

In an article in *Entertainment Weekly* in April [2009], [*Taking Woodstock* director Ang] Lee called Woodstock

> "Woodstock veterans . . . would take part in the huge Moratorium and Mobilization demonstrations against the Vietnam War."

"America's last moment of innocence." That's another cliché I think we can do without. That Woodstock comes down to us today as a symbol of innocence and reconciliation, a moment apart from the darker side of the 60s, is mostly an accident of historical memory, plus a little serendipity.

The Impact of Political Movements Before and After Woodstock

Woodstock was not a protest, and many of those attending never had attended, and never would, a political demonstration. (That applies to a couple of the friends with whom I attended the concert.) But without the political insurgencies that preceded it, without the vision of the possibility of change and self-definition that began with the civil-rights movement and was taken up by more and more Americans (students, women, and, earlier in that summer of 1969, gay people), Woodstock would never have happened. Richie Havens, in opening the festival, extemporized a song around one word: "I start strumming my guitar and the word 'freedom' comes out of my mouth as 'FREE-dom, FREE-dom' with a rhythm of its own," he would later recall. "This was the same feeling I'd been experiencing all along. The feeling that Bethel was such a special place, a moment when we all felt we were at the exact center of true freedom." No one listening to Havens's ode to freedom in 1969 could hear it without being reminded of Birmingham in 1963, Selma in 1965, and Martin Luther King Jr.'s martyrdom in 1968. Lang describes the Movement City that [social and political activist] Abbie Hoffman and other New York-based activists set up on the hillside, which came equipped with the usual movement paraphernalia: radical newspapers, leaflets, a mimeograph machine. All that proved unnecessary. As the days rolled by, Lang writes, "I noticed fewer and fewer people manning the Movement City booths set up by the various political organizations. The entire gathering had become Movement City."

The generational upheaval, of which Woodstock was one expression, had yet to reach its crest. A few months after the festival, in October and November 1969, many Woodstock veterans, and many others inspired by what they had heard about the gathering, would take part in the huge Moratorium and Mobilization demonstrations against the Vietnam War. And the following spring, in May 1970, they would be among the hundreds of thousands taking part in the national student strike following the invasion of Cambodia and the killings at Kent State University and Jackson State University.

The Movement City part of the Woodstock legacy tended to be forgotten in the years since, if not necessarily by the veterans, the musicians, or the organizers, than by Woodstock acolytes among succeeding generations. Certainly there was little of that legacy in evidence at the Woodstock commemorative concerts of 1994 and (especially) 1999. Woodstock is reduced in popular memory to a weekend of blissful abandon, a chance to dress up in flower-child trappings, a brief excursion to nirvana and back. Maybe on this 40th anniversary, at a moment when the country faces challenges and decisions every bit as important—and divisive—as in 1969, we can remember Woodstock as a more complicated, less "innocent" phenomenon. It was Eden, but it was also Gettysburg (or Agincourt,[2] as the *Times* would have it). And, thinking back, I still stand a-tiptoe at the memory.

Notes

1. Altamont is a speedway in Northern California where a rock music festival was held in December 1969. Members of the Hell's Angels motorcycle gang served as security guards. The festival was marred by violence, including one murder.
2. The Battle of Agincourt was a major English victory against a numerically superior French army in the Hundred Years' War.

The Woodstock Festival Site Has Historical and Cultural Significance Worth Commemorating

Michael William Doyle

The following viewpoint argues that the Woodstock music festival holds historical and cultural significance worth commemorating. The author asserts that despite the rain and shortages of food, water, and adequate sanitation, the event has always been seen as a success—the largest musical event of its time. Moreover, Woodstock has come to represent the countercultural movement, a significant era in American history. In fact, the crowd of nearly half a million young people—who endured despite the conditions—was a bigger story than the music, he maintains. The music was, however, one of the most impressive gatherings of talent in rock

---

SOURCE. Michael William Doyle, "Statement on the Historical and Cultural Significance of the 1969 Woodstock Festival Site," *Preliminary Draft Generic Environmental Impact Statement of the Bethel Performing Arts Center*, Allee King Rosen & Fleming, Inc. on behalf of the Gerry Foundation, September 25, 2001. Reproduced by permission of the Gerry Foundation.

music history. He concludes that Woodstock's impact is so significant that the word has become a part of the nation's cultural vocabulary. Michael William Doyle, PhD, teaches history at Ball State University in Indiana. This viewpoint is excerpted from a 2001 statement submitted on behalf of the Gerry Foundation, a corporation committed to building a museum at the original site of the festival in Bethel, New York.

The baffling history of mankind is full of obvious turning points and significant events: battles won, treaties signed, rulers elected or disposed, and now seemingly, planets conquered. Equally important are the great groundswells of popular movements that affect the minds and values of a generation or more, not all of which can be neatly tied to a time or place. Looking back upon the America of the '60s, future historians may well search for the meaning of one such movement. It drew the public's notice on the days and nights of Aug. 15 through 17, 1969, on the 600-acre farm of Max Yasgur in Bethel, N.Y.
—Time *magazine, August 29, 1969*

The Woodstock Music and Art Fair, held in the Catskill Mountains of New York's Sullivan County, showcased a veritable who's who of the top performers of rock, folk, and progressive popular music during the Sixties era. To this remote location was attracted an audience estimated variously at between a quarter- to a half-million mostly young people from all over the country. For the three summer days over which it was held, the Festival site was said to constitute the Empire State's second most populous city. The site itself had been selected by the Festival's organizers because it comprised a natural amphitheater that afforded decent acoustics and unobstructed sight views, plus plenty of space for camping on the grounds. To gauge the significance of the talent on stage, consider that over a third of the thirty-one groups or solo performers who played Woodstock have subsequently been inducted into the Rock and Roll Hall of Fame, with several more expected to be so honored in the coming years. Despite problems with the sound system, intermittent downpours, and critical shortages of food, drinking water, and toilet facilities, this self-billed "Aquarian Exposition" was universally regarded as a critical success. Even those who didn't attend reckoned it to be an epoch-making event, a gathering that has come to represent the acme of the era's counterculture. Recognizing its singular place in contemporary history, the U.S. Postal Service recently issued a first-class postage stamp in honor of Woodstock and based it on the distinctive dove-on-guitar neck design of the Festival's poster. Another indication of its importance is demonstrated by the inclusion of an entry for Woodstock in *The Dictionary of Cultural Literacy*, thus according it the status of a term that the scholars who compiled this reference work feel every educated member of our society would be expected to know.

> The Baby Boomers, who comprised most of the audience at the Festival, are frequently referred to as the 'Woodstock Generation.'

The Woodstock Festival site is significant for a number of reasons. First is its association as the setting for the largest musical event of its kind produced to that date. (And in this role, the land itself figuratively became an important and much remarked upon "player" in the drama that enfolded on its sylvan-fringed sward). Second, it is of local and regional significance because of the enormous impact, both immediate and lasting, the event had on the local and regional community. Finally, it is significant due to the symbolic weight with which the Festival and the Festival site have been invested by members of the Sixties counterculture, as well as their admirers and detractors over time. Indeed, this amorphous social movement subsequently came to be called "Woodstock Nation," and the Baby Boomers, who comprised most of the audience at the Festival, are frequently referred to as the "Woodstock Generation" as a result.

The Historic Context

The year preceding the Festival had been one of the most violent in post–World War II history. The long struggle for African-American civil rights had been forestalled following the assassination of its most articulate leader, the Reverend Martin Luther King, Jr. His murder had provoked rioting and arson in most of the nation's largest cities with the destruction of property worth hundreds of million dollars. Protests against American involvement in Vietnam had drawn thousands of people into the streets, most notably in Chicago the previous summer at the Democratic National Convention. There, demonstrators who, in their frustration at being prevented from picketing nearer the convention center, taunted law enforcement authorities and precipitated what the Kerner Commission report[1] later called a "police riot." A growing perception among women of their own lack of social and economic equality prompted the emergence of a new wave of feminism that in its insurgent stage went by the name of Women's Liberation. College campuses were convulsed with sit-ins opposing the Vietnam war and also against *in loco parentis*[2] practices. During the month before the Festival, a routine police raid on a gay bar in Greenwich Village touched off the Stonewall riots, which itself marked the birth of the Gay and Lesbian Liberation movement. All of these crises and disruptions to the status quo produced a feeling among many Americans, and particularly the youth, that the country was coming unraveled. Among the more radical segment of political and cultural activists on the left there was

Woodstock Introduces Santana's New Latin Sound to the World

Led by virtuoso guitarist Carlos Santana (1947–), the band Santana has been one of the most successful mainstream ethnic fusion acts in rock history, topping the charts since the 1960s with its signature blend of Latin and African sounds. Carlos Santana grew up to the distinctive mariachi sounds of his native Tijuana, Mexico. As a teenager in the 1950s, he became fascinated by the rhythm and blues and rock and roll sounds he heard on the radio. Upon learning to play guitar, he fused these disparate traditions into an exciting and unique sound that would later become his trademark.

In the mid-1960s, Santana moved to San Francisco, where he and other local musicians formed the Santana Blues Band, later shortened to Santana. The group—featuring Santana (guitar), Gregg Rolie (vocals and keyboards), Dave Brown (bass), Mike Shrieve (drums), Armando Peraza (percussion and vocals), Mike Carabello (percussion), and Jose Areas (percussion)—first gained recognition in the same dance halls that hosted psychedelic rock groups of the era such as the Grateful Dead and Jefferson Airplane. Santana's blend of Latin and African sounds was ill suited to the acid rock scene, but the group's frenetic performances captivated hippie audiences across the Bay Area. Under the direction of concert promoter Bill Graham, Santana landed a spot at the Woodstock Festival in New York, where the band's tour de force performance lodged Santana in the mainstream consciousness before the group had even recorded an album.

Santana released its first album, *Evil Ways*, in 1969. The title track from that debut effort reached the Top Ten—an unprecedented feat, given the song's overt Latin sound. The group's 1970 single "Black Magic Woman" enjoyed similar mass appeal and pushed the band's second album, Abraxas, to the top of the charts where it remained for six weeks. Santana III, released in 1971, likewise topped the charts and established Santana as a major force in the recording industry.

SOURCE. *Scott Tribble, "Santana," St. James Encyclopedia of Popular Culture, vol. 4, ed. by Sara Pendergast and Tom Pendergast. Detroit: St. James Press, 2000.*

an increasing sense that the next American revolution might be at hand. . . .

From Monterey to Woodstock

While groups such as the Haight-Ashbury Diggers [a radical community action group in San Francisco] helped organize free concerts in the San Francisco parks with the arrival of the "Summer of love" in 1967, a new type of musical gathering was being staged featuring acid rock groups and other eclectic performers whose talents ran from folk to jazz, and from soul to Indian classical music. The first of these was the Magic Mountain Festival held over a three-day period on Mount Tamalpais in Marin County across the Bay and north of San Francisco in early June 1967. It was followed about a week later by the much better known Monterey Pop Festival down the coast near Big Sur. Over a three-day period some 30,000 to 50,000 members of the "love generation" were treated to performances by British invasion groups such as the Who, soul singer Otis Redding, folkies like the Lovin' Spoonful and the Mamas and the Papas, as well as the Grateful Dead. Two of the breakout performances were by Janis Joplin and Big Brother and Jimi Hendrix with his band the Experience, who were making their American debut. Over the next two years several other festivals were held that aspired to replicate the critical success of the Monterey Pop Festival, and, their promoters hoped, to turn a profit. Although these festivals became more focused on the performers, their form—large numbers of people camping out on the grounds and together sharing close quarters—preserved the sense that they were sites where the counterculture itself was rehearsed, performed and, one might say, consumed, as at the be-ins.

The Woodstock Festival happened in a kind of backhanded way. Two young New York venture capitalists, John Roberts and Joel Rosenman placed an ad in the *New*

York Times stating simply "Two young men with unlimited capital looking for interesting, legitimate investment opportunities and business propositions." The ad immediately caught the eye of Michael Lang, a self-identified hippie rock promoter who had just organized his first festival with moderate success in Miami. He and his partner, Artie Kornfeld, were seeking financing to build a recording studio featuring all the latest technology in the Hudson River Valley town and bohemian enclave of Woodstock (Ulster County), N.Y. The town had been known as a haven for artists and writers since the turn of the century, and by the mid 1960's had begun to attract a host of well known musicians such as Bob Dylan and the Band. Lang and Kornfeld were convinced that a studio at Woodstock would attract their trade as well as musicians from all over the country. Messrs. Roberts and Rosenman were nonplussed by the pair's proposal, since they had already financed a recording studio and were looking now for new ventures to pursue. Lang and Kornfeld's prospectus had included the idea of staging a rock festival in advance of the studio's opening to both promote the studio and raise funds for its operation. That part of their proposal captured the investors' fancy and together the four men embarked upon the project of organizing a festival at Woodstock. . . .

> [Woodstock] featured the largest line-up of musical talent ever assembled and provided the largest live audience in history.

Why Woodstock Was Different

What made the 1969 Woodstock Festival different from all other rock festivals? The answer may be found in a combination of several factors: it featured the largest line-up of musical talent ever assembled and provided the largest live audience in history for them to showcase their talent. Several groups such as Sly and the Fam-

ily Stone; Santana; Crosby, Stills and Nash; and Richie Havens regarded their performances at Woodstock as career making. Another factor was the notable lack of violence among the festival goers. Medical personnel noted no injuries caused by violence, despite the plethora of deplorable conditions already documented. The number of people treated for adverse recreational drug reactions, reported by Dr. William Abruzzi, Festival Medical Director, was relatively small: around 800 cases in the three-day period, a minuscule figure in proportion to the size of the crowd (300,000–500,000) compared with later festivals that drew equal or smaller numbers of people. More than one commentator has remarked that the feeling of elan, bonhomie, and the spirit of cooperation that marked the Woodstock Festival was due in part to the prevalence of psychotropic substances rather than hard drugs such as methadrine, heroin, and cocaine, in addition to alcohol, which were much more in evidence at

Guitarist Carlos Santana (far left) has said that his performance at Woodstock was a pivotal moment in advancing his career. (Time & Life Pictures/Getty Images.)

subsequent festivals. A number of those gatherings were also marred by outbreaks of violence and rioting.

Because nothing had been organized on this scale before, the Woodstock Festival took on the aspect of a high stakes experiment where both the organizers and those in attendance grasped the need to improvise solutions to the many challenges they were faced with. Festival goers reported feeling a sense of accomplishment and exhilaration that together they found solutions to these challenges. Later festivals tended to be better organized because of the Woodstock experience and when they were not, crowds tended to be much less willing to put up with conditions they found wanting.

The Symbolic Importance of Woodstock

When talking about Woodstock's importance one needs to distinguish the event from the myth with which it is co-terminous. The myth of Woodstock was generated simultaneously with the event's unfolding and, like other cultural myths, has undergone periodic alterations and transformations down to the present time. In the strict sense of the term, myths are stories that are intended to convey larger truths which may not otherwise be verifiable; they may also provide explanations about the origins or meaning of phenomena whose facticity is beside the point. Social groups commonly create or recreate myths about themselves which serve to buttress cherished beliefs and values held by its members and signal how they collectively wish to be known. The myth of Woodstock is that in a time of military conflict abroad, racial and ethnic strife at home, when a deep social division known as the "generation gap" separated parents from children, a half a million mostly young people removed themselves from proximity to these conflicts and went "back to the garden" to "try and set [their] soul[s] free." Attracted by the largest lineup of popular music talent ever showcased at one venue, these young people endured inclement weather, and critical shortages of food, water, shelter, dry clothing, and sanitation facilities; in sum, most of the basic necessities of life. Despite these hardships, for three days they lived peaceably in a state of harmony and love, sharing what limited resources they had with one another. Written and verbal accounts of those who have undertaken self-described "pilgrimages" to the Festival site indicate that they do so as a way of feeling the "vibrations" that are said to inhere in the land in the aftermath of this mass ceremonial experience.

The Long-Term Significance of Woodstock

In 1969, rock critic Ellen Sander appraised the immediate impact of the Festival this way: "No longer can the magical multicolored phenomenon of pop culture be overlooked or underrated. It's happening everywhere, but now it has happened in one place at one time so hugely that it was indeed historic. . . . The audience was a much bigger story than the groups. It was major entertainment news that the line-up of talent was of such magnificence and magnitude (thirty-one acts, nineteen of which were colossal). . . . These were, however, the least significant events of what happened over the Woodstock weekend. What happened was that the largest number of people ever assembled for any event other than a war lived together, intimately and meaningfully and with such natural good cheer that they turned on not only everyone surrounding them but the mass media, and, by extension, millions of others, young and old, particularly many elements hostile to the manifestations and ignorant of the substance of pop culture."

> " Woodstock . . . helped establish what only two years before had been underground or avant-garde musical styles and ushered them into the mainstream. "

Woodstock was the culmination of a transformation in American popular music that had begun with Monterey. The Monterey Pop Festival introduced the emerging acid rock bands of the San Francisco Bay Area to a wider audience estimated at 50,000 people as well as to influential record executives and producers from New York and Los Angeles. Woodstock introduced the same wide diversity of talent, albeit on an expanded scale, to a truly mass audience. And not just to those who attended the Festival. A subsequent documentary film (the Academy Award-winning, 3-hour long *Woodstock*, directed by Michael Wadleigh and released in March 1970) and several sound recordings helped establish what only two years before had been underground or avant-garde musical styles and ushered them into the mainstream.

The Festival's Impact on Music

Participating musicians, industry insiders, and rock critics and historians concur that Woodstock changed the way that popular music was programmed and marketed. Festival promoters noted the large numbers of fans who were willing to put up with often inadequate facilities and the number of festivals for a time increased after Woodstock. Promoters saw opportunities to improve their profit margin by more efficiently organizing festivals, including by placing stringent controls over the collection of tickets at the gate. . . . They also understood that increased ticket prices would need to be offset by offering better sanitation and protection from inclement weather. By the mid-1970s these ends were realized by moving the festivals from pastoral settings into sports arenas and convention centers and limiting the shows to a single-day or evening. From the audience's standpoint, the provision of fixed seats, and assigned and price-segmented locations fundamentally altered the festival-going experience, diminishing the egalitarianism that had been a hallmark of the outdoor festivals. Likewise, the shift from multi-day festivals where fans camped on the site to one-day concerts limited the amount of bonding between fans and thereby diminished the sense of community that many commentators considered the *sine qua non* of the Woodstock experience.

The development of "arena rock" marked the end of the rock "vaudeville circuit," and led to the demise of the smaller concert hall venues (those having a capacity of a few thousand people) that had been the incubator of new musical styles. Several of them closed in 1970–1971, including the Boston Tea Party and Bill Graham's Fillmores' West and East, in San Francisco and New York respectively. The arenas also gave the upper hand to the style of music called heavy metal, represented by loudly amplified guitar based and blues-inflected bands composed almost entirely of white male musicians, whose aggressive style of playing was ideally suited for filling the audible space in arena settings.

> The Yasgur Farm site will no doubt maintain its vaunted status as the authentic location of one of the Sixties' most celebrated events.

After Woodstock, musicians apprehended the seemingly insatiable demand for their music and began commanding higher fees. It thus soon proved to be no longer economically feasible to book several major bands on the same bill and keep ticket prices within an acceptable range while maintaining profitability. This in turn led to the segmentation of the fan base. At Monterey and Woodstock, the programming of groups representing numerous genres exposed audiences to many different musical styles at the same time, thereby giving them a keener appreciation of American popular music in all its diversity. In the years following Woodstock, however, fans were channeled into attending concerts that featured fewer acts, typically representing one or two musical styles. . . .

What is apparent . . . is that although the original Festival can never be duplicated, the very notion of Woodstock retains an enduring grip upon many people's imagination. Woodstock as an idea is portable. Indeed, the 1969 Festival had been shifted from place to place in search of a site, before landing in Bethel. While festivals bearing the Woodstock name may continue to be held elsewhere, and succeed by drawing on the cache of the original Aquarian Exposition, the Yasgur Farm site will no doubt maintain its vaunted status as the authentic location of one of the Sixties' most celebrated events.

Note

1. This refers to the findings of the National Advisory Commission on Civil Disorders, established by President Lyndon Johnson to investigate a spate of race riots between 1965 and 1967. It was chaired by Illinois governor Otto Kerner.
2. A Latin term meaning "in place of the parent." Prior to countercultural opposition in the 1960s, undergraduate students were subject to many restrictions on their private lives. For example, women were subject to curfews and risked expulsion from some colleges if deemed morally undesirable. Some universities restricted freedom of speech, often forbidding organizations from demonstrating on campus.

Views on the Legacy of Woodstock Vary Significantly

Jerry Shriver

In the viewpoint that follows, a music writer asserts that forty years after the Woodstock music festival, opinions on its relevance vary considerably. Indeed, while some readers polled by *USA Today* see Woodstock as a peaceful paradise and inspiration for change, others speak of hedonism and an epic disaster filtered by the media. Sam Yasgur, son of the late Max Yasgur, who leased his farm for the festival, views Woodstock as an expression of basic rights. Rock critic Dave Marsh views Woodstock more cynically as "some slick guys figuring out how to make a buck off . . . the social vision of the '60s." Whatever Woodstock means and whether to keep it alive will depend on America's national identity. Jerry Shriver is a music critic for *USA Today*.

SOURCE. Jerry Shriver, "Woodstock at 40: Does It Still Matter?" *USA Today*, August 14, 2009. Copyright 2009, USA Today. Reproduced by permission.

F olk singer Tim Hardin stood before the gathering multitudes at Woodstock on Aug. 15, 1969, and asked in his opening song, "How can we hang on to a dream?"

Forty years later, a response comes from Maggie Zmigrodski, 60, and Waverly Zmigrodski, 8, as they emerge from a psychedelically decorated bus in the museum that now hugs the site of the four-day festival that drew about 450,000 people here and helped define the Baby Boomer generation.

"When you get home, Dad will have to Google 'tie-dye' to show you how to do it," Maggie tells her granddaughter. Waverly nods at the teachable moment and they head toward the *Impact of Woodstock* exhibit.

It's a start.

Questioning the Relevance of Woodstock

Woodstock marks a milestone anniversary this weekend [August 2009] with two relatively small-scale concerts here—one featuring multiple Woodstock veterans is expected to draw about 14,000—and a few modest celebrations around the world.

> [The fortieth anniversary] resurrects questions of whether Woodstock's organic, peace-and-love-through-music legacy still resonates.

It all resurrects questions of whether Woodstock's organic, peace-and-love-through-music legacy still resonates—and whether it's relevant to young people living in a high-tech, marketing-driven era of splintered musical tastes, widely diverse political views and short attention spans.

Woodstock anniversaries have come and gone, but now there's a whiff of urgency: More than one-third of the 32 acts that performed during the Woodstock Music & Art Fair on Max Yasgur's farm have lost members (Hardin died of a drug overdose in 1980).

The peers of the hundreds of thousands of young people who slogged through the traffic and mud here are heading into retirement. And their offspring and *their* offspring—without anything as unifying as the dread of the military draft—are more diverse in their interests.

The Historical Record

This time around, the historical record is more accessible than ever. The $100 million-plus Bethel Woods Center for the Arts—comprising a museum dedicated to Woodstock and the '60s, an outdoor stage and the preserved concert site—opened here last summer [2008]. It has drawn more than 70,000 visitors to its relatively out-of-the-way location a little more than 100 miles northwest of New York City.

Among recent tourists: a peace-through-music activist from Taiwan and a Chinese protester who was jailed after the pro-democracy uprising in Beijing's Tiananmen Square in 1989.

"Happens every day," says museum director Wade Lawrence, who wants to broaden the center's mission into a think tank for 1960s ideals. "A lot of people with different connections want to be involved."

A slew of live recordings, many never released, are being rolled out. They include a six-CD set, *40 Years On: Back to Yasgur's Farm*. Today, Sirius XM radio launches the limited-run Woodstock Channel, featuring music and interviews.

Nearly a dozen books, including the first in-depth account from co-founder Michael Lang, join the four dozen already in print. More than two hours of never-before-seen footage have been added to a new DVD version of the Oscar-winning documentary *Woodstock: 3 Days of Peace & Music*.

> At the extremes, Woodstock was either the peaceful 'paradise' described in Joni Mitchell's song—or an alfalfa field turned disaster area.

Meanwhile, Ang Lee's *Taking Woodstock*, a comedy based on behind-the-scenes events, opens Aug. 26. Sony and Woodstock Ventures, the founding group that owns the trademark and continues to create Woodstock projects, have relaunched Woodstock.com as a social networking site. And lines of T-shirts, tie-dyed fashions and paper dolls are keeping the festival's fashion legacy alive.

But the interpretation of that record and debates about what, if anything, will be remembered decades hence still can spark mud fights. (Or apathy: A June 5 posting on the Woodstock.com forums section asking "Does anybody even care any more?" has received zero responses.)

A Diversity of Opinions

The diversity of opinions expressed by festival attendees and participants, museum visitors, bloggers and readers queried by *USA Today* is as wide as the generation gap in the '60s and the red-blue political divide of today.

At the extremes, Woodstock was either the peaceful "paradise" described in Joni Mitchell's song—or an alfalfa field turned disaster area without adequate food, shelter and sanitation. A media-inflated mirage and marketing vehicle, or inspiration for change. A free, mass counterculture expression at its most harmonious, or a hedonistic symbol of "selfishness . . . indulgence . . . and the drug problem," as former [President Ronald] Reagan attorney general Ed Meese says in a video exhibit at the museum.

Or something in between. Or nothing at all.

"Woodstock never mattered," asserts *USA Today* reader Cody McCormick, 50, of Carrollton, Ga.

"What is this fascination?" asks reader Mark Stallings, 39, of Colorado Springs. "Move on. The romanticized ideal . . . deserves to rest in peace."

Just wait, says festival co-founder Lang, 65, who canceled plans for a free anniversary concert in Brooklyn when he couldn't find sponsors. "A lot of those seeds

planted in the Woodstock era are beginning to flower," Lang says. "From the green movement to sustainable development and organic gardening, all these things seem to be coming back to us."

Love and Togetherness

Some under age 20 support Lang's view.

After seeing the museum exhibits, young Waverly of Cazenovia, N.Y., concludes that the meaning of Woodstock is that she and her generation "could accomplish something if we tried."

Robert Kreis, 18, of Dunmore, Pa., standing with his dad, Joe, 47, before the commemorative marker at the concert site, loves the "passion in the music" but doubts a Woodstock could happen with his generation.

Festival attendee Robin "Blue" Hallock poses with a photo of herself taken forty years earlier at Woodstock. Today opinions vary over how important the event was or what it meant culturally. (**Associated Press.**)

"Three days of no problems and no violence? No." But a mass gathering to effect change in an area such as the environment "would be worth a try," he says.

To Gabe Toledo, 17, of Stuart, Fla., Woodstock "represents true freedom. I'm sure (the people who were there) believe it's something that everyone should experience. Not the drugs or whatever, but the whole peace, love and togetherness idea. It's important and I don't see why someone would disagree."

He'll see when age provides a broader perspective, says Schon Zwakman, 34, of Cottage Grove, Minn. "Sure (Woodstock matters), if only for the chance to wring additional revenue from the generation that attended it and the successive generations of college students who want to participate in vicarious nostalgia. . . . (It) was a historically great music festival, period."

Jefferson Airplane guitarist Paul Kantner, 68, who played the festival (and will play with Jefferson Starship at Saturday's concert here), echoes that sentiment. "Nobody went to Woodstock to make a statement. We just all accidentally showed up. It was a good time in the country, it wasn't a protest."

Still, says John Fogerty, who played the festival with Creedence Clearwater Revival, Woodstock represented youths united by opposition to the Vietnam War and a commitment to civil rights—a generation "feeling its voice at a singular moment."

But that voice was co-opted by commercial interests, and "folks like [social and political activist] Abbie Hoffman who wanted to ride on the coattails take credit (for the ideals). . . . When Yuppies and Reagan Democrats came along, I'd say, 'Where's my Woodstock generation?' . . . A lot of that original fervor has been lost. Perhaps I made it more important than it really was."

The staging of Woodstock, haphazard as it was, remains important because it influences every large concert and festival staged today, says Perry Farrell, 50, who in 1991 founded Lollapalooza, which drew more than 75,000 to Chicago last weekend.

"At the time, Woodstock was one of the few models you could look at for massive music gatherings," he says. "Today it's so organized. We have learned so many lessons—we've changed the business and production structure to better handle traffic, food and water."

For a generation accustomed to well-produced festivals, Woodstock is "an interesting curio to read about," says Justin Gage, 34, founder of the music blog Aquarium Drunkard and a program director for Sirius XM. "Now there are so many festivals, it seems pretty commonplace. Were people going to Woodstock for change or to party and listen to music? I think it's more of the latter."

The End of Innocence

Rock critic Dave Marsh, 59, editor of *Creem* magazine in 1969 and author of a tough Woodstock critique in the August/September [2009] issue of *Relix* music magazine, views the festival, which he chose not to attend, as an example of "some slick guys figuring out how to make a buck off . . . the social vision of the '60s. . . . It was the end of innocence.

"It wasn't utopian," he adds. "Utopia has plumbing. It wasn't idyllic. Woodstock is important because it was big. And a culture that says big is best is the culture that is strangling our economy, and the culture Michael Jackson died of. It's an unhealthy culture, to say the least."

Rona Roberts, 64, widow of festival co-founder John Roberts and a Woodstock attendee, is saddened by such judgments. "I would hate to think the legacy was just, 'Oh, yeah, a big music concert.' I would hope it remains more of a concept of youth and community and

> "What Woodstock was in the final analysis was an expression of some very basic rights we sometimes take for granted—the right to gather, the right to criticize, the right to dress funny, the right to listen to your own music."

shared values and a spirit of caring, a sense of being in it together."

Another festival co-founder, Joel Rosenman, 66, a partner in Woodstock Ventures, vows to "never lose sight of our heritage. We're not so much about celebrating the event of '69 but in carrying the spirit forward."

He won't say how much money the Woodstock name generates, only that "it has never been a financial bonanza. Woodstock is not the pot of gold at the end of the rainbow. It's the rainbow."

Ultimately, the meaning of Woodstock and the necessity of keeping it alive relate to our national identity, according to the son of the farmer who owned the land where the rainbow met the mud 40 years ago.

Says Sam Yasgur, 67, son of the late Max Yasgur and now the Sullivan County Attorney: "What Woodstock was in the final analysis was an expression of some very basic rights we sometimes take for granted—the right to gather, the right to criticize, the right to dress funny, the right to listen to your own music.

"When we lose those, we lose what we're all about."

Advertisers Use Woodstock Nostalgia to Target Baby Boomers

Amy Jacques

The following viewpoint argues that nostalgia comes when people see parallels between the day's uncertainties and those in the past. Indeed, the author asserts, parallels can be drawn between 1969 and 2009. In both years, the United States was involved in unpopular wars. In 1969, baby boomers, those born between 1945 and 1964, feared the draft. In 2009, they faced threats to their incomes due to the financial crisis and the downturn in the economy. Many advertisers have targeted baby boomers using the appeal of nostalgia—marketing Woodstock as a simpler, idyllic time, according to the author. However, she suggests, industry analysts differ on the rebranding of Woodstock. While some feel rebranding does not diminish the significance of the event, others argue that parallels between 1969 and 2009 are dubious and

SOURCE. Amy Jacques, "Take a Trip: Looking Backward and Forward at 'Brand Woodstock,'" *Public Relations Tactics*, vol. 16, August 2009, p. 14. © 2010 The Public Relations Society of America. Reproduced by permission of Public Relations Tactics.

minimize the festival's importance. Amy Jacques is associate editor of *Tactics*, a public relations trade magazine.

P eace signs. Mud people. Psychedelic music. Bohemian clothing. Flower power.

These terms continue to symbolize more than a three-day festival as this August [2009] marks the 40th anniversary of the Woodstock Music and Art Fair, which featured the likes of Jimi Hendrix, The Who, Janis Joplin, Santana and Jefferson Airplane. Rather, the words evoke a sense of nostalgia for the larger idea of "Woodstock Nation."

"It was the moment that the counterculture was branded in marketing terms," says longtime *Rolling Stone* contributor and music critic Anthony DeCurtis. "The notion of Woodstock Nation indicated a demographic niche as much as anything else."

Woodstock took place during a period of political, social and economic unrest for the United States. When reflecting on 1969, the dark reality of the times is called to mind, including the Vietnam War, the draft, civil rights challenges and protests.

Parallels can be drawn today with the current financial crisis, the economic downturn and the unpopular wars in Iraq and Afghanistan. It seems that nostalgia for the past occurs when the underlying cause remains relevant in modern times—and can overshadow the problems of the day.

"Woodstock's success was born from the widespread discontentment of that time and the notion that 'the system' was failing the populous," says Patrick Schwerdtfeger, author of *Make Yourself Useful: Your Guide to the 21st Century* and founder of the Tactical Execution company. He notes that today's economy has "left Americans with similar feelings, making the events of 1969 equally relevant in today's world."

An Excess of Memorabilia

Looking around, there is a plethora of Woodstock-related memorabilia surfacing. This summer marks the release of three Woodstock-related films including Ang Lee's *Taking Woodstock*, at least 13 books, such as *The Road to Woodstock* written by festival co-founder Michael Lang (who is also working on a VH1/History Channel documentary) and numerous CD releases, re-releases and compilation discs by artists who played at the original festival. In addition, Warner Home Video will release a

A 2009 Grammy Awards after-party featured performers in "Woodstock" attire. A wide variety of Woodstock references and memorabilia have surfaced inviting comparisons of today's political climate to the social uncertainties of 1969. (Getty Images.)

Musical Artists Who Did Not Appear at Woodstock

- Although his back-up group, The Band, played to the massive audience, Bob Dylan never made it, as one of his children was hospitalized that weekend.

- Joni Mitchell, who wrote a song about the festival, based her lyrics on what she learned about the festival from her then-boyfriend Graham Nash. She did not attend Woodstock at the advice of her manager, who recommended she appear on the *Dick Cavett Show* instead.

- John Lennon wanted to be a part of Woodstock, but he was in Canada and the US government refused him an entry visa.

- Iron Butterfly got stuck at the airport and the helicopter booked to ferry them to the site failed to arrive. Organizers were also said to be worried that the band's heavy metal music would incite violence.

SOURCE. *Woodstockstory.com; and Spencer Bright, "Forty Far-Out Facts You Never Knew About Woodstock,"* Daily Mail *(UK), August 8, 2009.*

four-hour director's cut of *Woodstock: 3 Days of Peace and Music*. And Rhino will put out a six-CD box set of Woodstock performances.

As if that's not enough, there is a "Heroes of Woodstock" national tour and a special concert celebration on the site of the original festival at the Bethel Woods Center for the Arts in upstate New York, featuring some of the performers from 1969. The trademark event poster with the dove on a guitar neck has been repurposed numerous times, even as part of a clothing line that Target recently launched in conjunction with Woodstock. The Rock and Roll Hall of Fame has a special exhibit honoring the 40th anniversary. And Woodstock.com plans to re-launch itself as a social networking site.

The Appeal of Nostalgia

A large portion of advertising in the United States today uses the nostalgia appeal—and it is evident that the 1960s are popular right now, notes Dr. Michael Solomon, a marketing professor at Saint Joseph's University in Philadelphia. A financial ad features Dennis Hopper from "Easy Rider," the tag line for "The Bachelorette" is the "summer of love," Luvs diapers feature the VW Microbus, Volkswagen is juxtaposing its newer models with the classic Beetle and countless clothing lines are showcasing a return to bohemia with throwbacks to fringe, headbands and peace signs.

Several things are fueling this: the recession and looking at the past idealistically when times are tough, the election of [Barack] Obama as the new president and a resurgence of idealism, the large number of baby boomers in the current population and young people's acceptance of the branding of a culture—and embracing "the remix of old classics," according to Solomon.

> Marketing nostalgia can . . . be dangerous as it is such a personal emotion.

And this idea of remixing old classics is making a comeback in advertising and marketing, Stuart Elliott reported for *The New York Times* in April. To help ease consumers' minds about the recession, marketers are trying to appeal to fond memories to help sell products.

"It's about yearning for the past, a simpler time, even though the 1960s and 1970s were not simple," Frank

Cooper, chief marketing officer for sparkling beverages at the Pepsi-Cola North America Beverages unit of PepsiCo, told the *Times*. "They just seem simple, looking back."

Vintage packaging, formulas, jingles and slogans are cropping up everywhere from McDonald's to General Mills cereal boxes to Coca-Cola soft drinks. And hard times have often inspired a look back to happier moments. This is not a novel concept—World War II also experienced a nostalgia boom as seen with movies like "Meet Me in St. Louis" and songs like "Long Ago and Far Away," Elliott adds.

But marketing nostalgia can also be dangerous as it is such a personal emotion. "Often-times the things that we find nostalgic are so unique and idiosyncratic that they need no packaging for the effect," says musicologist and Syracuse University professor Theo Cateforis. "They speak to us directly. If one tries to force that emotional connection, then it can often seem manipulative."

> Academics, music and culture critics and PR and marketing professionals remain divided regarding the wisdom of the branding and re-branding of Woodstock.

Cateforis goes on to explain that part of Woodstock's impact on history is that it solidified the connection between the 1960s and protest music. "Woodstock forever stamped rock music as a genre whose authenticity could be measured by its social relevance," he says.

Analysts Are Divided on Branding

However, academics, music and culture critics and PR and marketing professionals remain divided regarding the wisdom of the branding and re-branding of Woodstock.

"I don't think Woodstock was ever about celebrity, and it's certainly not about that now, even with all of the anniversary products/projects being marketed to cash in on it one more time," says Jeff Tamarkin, who has been writing about music for more than 25 years and is currently the associate editor of *JazzTimes*. "As so many have pointed out, it's always been about the event itself, the notion of half a million people coming together and expressing themselves as one."

And the infamous "Dean of Rock Critics" Robert Christgau was not interested in acknowledging the anniversary and declined to comment to *Tactics* on the topic altogether.

"People who are likely to pay for Woodstock memorabilia are doing so because they see a lack in today's rock music, as well as in the culture surrounding the music," Cateforis adds. "Part of the nostalgia is rooted in the mythical belief that rock at that time was akin to folk music, which is to say that it was impervious to market forces, and sprung from the voices of a youth generation."

Woodstock Still Resonates

Regardless, it is clear that Woodstock still resonates with the population. Whether it's the nostalgia appeal, an appreciation for the music of that generation or just an interest in history, people who were at the original festival and those who may be learning about it for the first time feel strongly about Woodstock in one way or another—and the brand still holds weight after many years.

"I wasn't at Woodstock. So for me, as for most people, my experience of the event is mediated almost entirely through the movie, which I still find thrilling," says rock scribe Richard Gehr, a former editor at *Spin* magazine and regular contributor to *The Village Voice*. "The persistent re-

> Rather than consider dubious parallels between 1969 and 2009, I'd prefer [the promoters] to simply let it be.

branding of the event, however, is bothersome. Rather than consider dubious parallels between 1969 and 2009,

I'd prefer [the promoters] to simply let it be, as it were, so people can enjoy that remarkable event in all its historical specificity."

The Spontaneity of Woodstock Cannot Be Reproduced

Jason Laure

Despite several attempts, promoters have been unable to re-create the spirit of the 1969 Woodstock music festival, argues the author of the following viewpoint. What happened at the original Woodstock was spontaneous, he claims. Most of the young people who traveled to Woodstock learned about the festival by word of mouth, and the unexpected numbers forced promoters to make the festival free. The festival was not meant to be a demonstration, he asserts, yet the generational divide of the time led nearly a half million young people to travel across the United States to gather in one place, hoping to change the world. Nevertheless, it was not the beginning of an era, but the end, never to be duplicated, he concludes. Jason Laure is a photojournalist and the creator of a number of iconic images of Woodstock.

SOURCE. Jason Laure, "Memory of a Free Festival," *The World & I Online*, vol. 14, August 1999, p. 232. Copyright 1999 News World Communications, Inc. Reproduced by permission.

I arrived in San Francisco at the end of the summer of love in 1967 and stayed for six months in Haight-Ashbury. We would gather in Golden Gate Park for free concerts by the Grateful Dead and Jefferson Airplane. It was there that I bought my first camera and started photographing these folks. Nearly two years later in New York, the idea of seeing old friends and meeting new ones brought me to Woodstock.

A Spontaneous Event

When it began, no one could have known that the Woodstock Rock Festival—a three-day celebration of community and music—would turn into a watershed moment of American culture and a landmark of the twentieth century. Woodstock defined a generation and symbolized the differences between the World War II generation and their children. It was the largest peaceful gathering in our history, and it happened spontaneously.

Woodstock grew to half a million by word of mouth alone. Most of us heard about it from like-minded friends and simply picked up our backpacks and went. We weren't concerned about where we would sleep, how we would live, or any of the other mundane details. We were drawn by the promise of the music—the music that defined us and that still endures thirty years later. From all over the country we made our way to the tiny town of Bethel (there was no place for the festival in Woodstock proper). Fortunately, a local farmer named Max Yasgur offered his land to the organizers, giving the event a home.

Woodstock literally stopped traffic. For the only time in its history, the New York State Thruway was closed down by sheer volume. Undaunted, hippies simply left their cars on what was the best-paved parking lot around and walked the rest of the way to the site. The performers had to be helicoptered in; there was no other way in or out.

Photo on previous page: Attendance at Woodstock far outstripped what the organizers anticipated, causing traffic jams that shut down the New York State Thruway. (Getty Images.)

Although tickets were sold, the endless stream of people arriving gave the organizers no choice but to let them in free of charge—and it became a free festival. This was very much in keeping with the ethos of the participants: share everything, experience life, and "don't sweat the small stuff."

The Heart of Woodstock

Music was at the heart of Woodstock. An endless roster of the best in the business performed day and night. Music was the common bond that transcended professional status, religion, education, and region. It brought us together as a community ready to change the world.

> There have been attempts to re-create the spirit of Woodstock, but the defining spontaneity of that free festival remains elusive.

Though often characterized by the slogan "make love, not war," Woodstock wasn't an overt demonstration. There weren't any posters or rallies; it all came out through the music. Hundreds of thousands of draft-age people were facing a war that seemed it would never end. The festival gave them hope. Young people from small towns could see that there were half a million others just like them who were facing the same thing.

Although people watching from the outside thought it was the beginning of an era, it was in fact the end. Those of us who had lived through the summer of love kept hearing about an "end of summer" event in the East. We all wanted to be there. Woodstock was to mark the culmination of that era and the end of a decade.

Since 1969, there have been attempts to re-create the spirit of Woodstock, but the defining spontaneity of that free festival remains elusive.

The Woodstock 1994 Festival Reflects Cultural Changes

Stephen Rodrick

In the following satirical viewpoint, journalist Stephen Rodrick, currently a contributing editor for *Men's Journal* and *New York Magazine*, points out significant cultural changes evident in the Woodstock 1994 musical festival. Marketing, not music, seemed to be the primary goal of Woodstock 1994, he argues. While Woodstock 1969 promoters promised "Three Days of Peace and Music," the unofficial slogan of Woodstock 1994, Rodrick claims, became "Woodstock '94: Where the Pepsi Costs More Than the Pot." Indeed, a slice of pizza cost $11 and a product-tie-in bottle of iced tea $6. The crowd at Woodstock 1994 was far less peaceful than were the swaying hippies at Woodstock 1969, he maintains. The number requiring treatment for injuries was so great that the medical director claimed treating the wounded in Vietnam was easier. One day, thirsty fans chanting "Liberate the Pepsi" over-ran a concession stand, giving the sponsors their due, Rodrick concludes.

SOURCE. Stephen Rodrick, "Gone to Pot," *The New Republic*, vol. 211, September 5, 1994, p. 9. Copyright © 1994 by The New Republic, Inc. Reproduced by permission of *The New Republic*.

A naked man weaves dreamily back and forth. It is 5 A.M. at Woodstock '94, and 350,000 of us are either extras in a Francis Ford Coppola film or vacationing at a hipster detention camp. A mist falls over the minimum-security site, glistening in the headlights of sanitation trucks enforcing the blurry line between walking in mud and walking in human waste. The main stage flickers with strobe lights as electronic bands bleat out their apocalyptic bebop. Despite the hour and the permissive atmosphere, the naked man draws a crowd. I reach the fellow . . . and ask the inevitable: Why are you unclothed? After a moment, the man focuses his glassy eyes and whispers, Charlie Manson-like: "Because I can't afford the T-shirts!"

The Marketing Excess

[Playwright and novelist] Thornton Wilder once said nothing succeeds like excess. If so, then we've just witnessed the most successful event since the marketing of The Flinstones. By the time I got to Woodstock [there] were a half-million two-liter product-tie-in bottles of Lipton Brisk Ice Tea strong—and they all cost $6. "WOODSTOCK '94: WHERE THE PEPSI COSTS MORE THAN THE POT" quickly became the unofficial slogan of the thirsty masses.

> Behind the stage, sheltered from the rain and the hoi polloi, hospitality tents are serving up feasts.

Not that everyone is paying. Behind the stage, sheltered from the rain and the hoi polloi ["the masses"], hospitality tents are serving up feasts finer than the $11 "peace" of pizza available outside. With its pastel couches and comfy chairs, the Pepsico palace looks as if somebody's trucked in furniture from the Hamptons. More than premium ice cream is available for the Haagen Dazs dudes. "We had steak and shrimp last night; even for me, that was a little crass," said one distributor, rubbing his ample tummy.

"You get going through the frog's mouth and then you come out its ass and swim around with this chick. It was O.K." That's how one teen with an H.R. Haldeman fade cut describes a ride through Peter Gabriel's video motion simulator called Mindblender. It sounds pretty interesting, but the two capsules are suspiciously shaped and decorated like huge cans of Mountain Dew and Ocean Spray cranberry juice. When the pod doors open, you half-expect carbonated liquid to gurgle out. I am in the Surreal Field, an area dedicated to the "interactive generation." Somebody goofed, because it is actually the

Attendees at Woodstock '94 take shelter underneath a billboard for one of the festival's sponsors. The 1994 festival emphasized marketing and product tie-ins far more than the 1969 event. (**WireImage**.)

interadvertising generation they're targeting. Let's see, should I go get a completely removable Apple Computer tattoo? Ride the Butterfinger Bender? Or reminisce at the Pepsi-sponsored Jimi Hendrix museum?

From Hippies to Terrorists

Fortunately, the vulgarity of the privileged attendees and the products they're hawking is not present among the youth of America. Unfortunately, neither is originality or solicitude. As the rain pours down, one hill becomes a muddy amusement tool. A group of kids who don't know Wavy Gravy from Gravy Train plunges headlong into a stagnant pond of mud and name-brand trash. "Now we look like those people from the Woodstock movie!" says one, triumphantly. They slap hands and head back to their tents. Mission accomplished.

> Somehow, America has moved from swaying hippies to forearm-shivering junior terrorists.

"Kill The Press! Kill The Press!" The chanting grows louder as Nine Inch Nails prepares to take the stage. Apparently, photographers are encroaching on the merry band of lunatics in the mosh pit (or the "moosh pit," as the rapidly calcifying Joe Cocker called it). It seems body slamming to Melissa Etheridge doing Janis Joplin tunes has left them in a bad mood. Somehow, America has moved from swaying hippies to forearm-shivering junior terrorists. Nowhere was this clearer than in the stage announcements. No longer were there calls to watch out for the brown acid. Instead: "Todd, meet your friends by the MTV booth—they have your Ritalin."

Casualties of Aggressive Behavior

The more aggressive behavior has its price. During peak business hours—while Aerosmith and Metallica are performing—casualties are coming in at a rate of one every twenty seconds. "It was better in Vietnam," says medical director Dr. Ferdinand Anderson. "You knew what kind of injuries you were getting." All night long, a steady stream of ambulances—their sirens off, lest they disturb the revelers—heads for local hospitals. Many of the injured do not go gently. One straw-haired thrasher, resplendent in mud, beer and a neck brace, expresses himself rather inarticulately: "Let go of me, you f-----' f---ers. I'm going to f-----' f--- you up if you don't get me out of this f---er." When he sees me writing, he gives me the finger. Only then does he smile. I tell him to have a nice night.

> The rash of injuries surprises members of the press . . . watching the teeming horde play involuntary Twister in the muck.

The rash of injuries surprises members of the press, many of whom remain under a tent fitted with two massive monitors, watching the teeming horde play involuntary Twister in the muck. "We're broadcasting live from Woodstock," says a radio reporter as he holds his microphone up to the speaker. Part of the laziness is bitterness. The press is routinely denied access to the musicians because it is "too crowded" backstage. Yet many a rock critic sees 15-year-olds with Pepsi passes sliding by to meet and greet with Bob Dylan. Apparently to be media is human, to hawk soft drinks is divine.

Alas, even conglomerates get their comeuppance. On Saturday freedom fighters chanting "Liberate the Pepsi, Liberate the Pepsi" overran an undermanned concession stand. By Sunday afternoon, as the pressed khaki, Louis Vuitton-schlepping crowd is heading for home, Pepsi drones load the plush furniture onto a moving van: the tent has been requisitioned as a second field hospital for the battered and frozen. "It was the least we could do," explains one publicist. "Pepsi's done here." Uh-huh.

CHAPTER 3

Personal Narratives

A Woman Shares Her Woodstock Experience as a Teen

Susan Reynolds

In the following firsthand account, a teen during the summer of 1969 tells her Woodstock story. She left home to live with her sister because her family was fiercely divided on the Vietnam War—one brother was a veteran, the other a conscientious objector. After hearing about the festival on the radio, she, her sister, her sister's boyfriend, and her brother the conscientious objector joined the pilgrimage to Woodstock. While she did not smoke marijuana, Reynolds admits that the air was heavy with marijuana smoke and warnings about bad acid (LSD), but she felt safe, nevertheless. She describes the antiwar sentiment and explains that the music bound them all together. Woodstock changed how she viewed the world and led her to join others in actively opposing the Vietnam War. Susan Reynolds is the editor of *Woodstock Revisited*, a volume of firsthand accounts from which this viewpoint is taken.

Photo on previous page: A hippie couple stand together at Woodstock. **(Time & Life Pictures/Getty Images.)**

SOURCE. Susan Reynolds, *Woodstock Revisited*, edited by Susan Reynolds, Avon, MA: Adams Media, 2009. Copyright © 2009 by Susan Reynolds. Reproduced by permission.

Because my family was as divided as our country at the time (one brother had fought in Vietnam; the other threatened to move to Canada) and I was an antsy teenager, I leapt at any chance to escape the arguments at home and the sleepy town on the banks of the Allegheny River where we lived. Thus, I spent the summer of 1969 living with my sister (who was fresh out of airline school) and her three female roommates in a cramped one-bedroom apartment in Queens [New York City].

Joining the Pilgrimage

When local radio stations in New York began advertising several outdoor rock festivals, Rozanne, our brother, Roy (the conscientious objector), and I set our sights on the Woodstock festival. We had not prepurchased tickets and had little real idea of what we would encounter.

Nevertheless, the three of us, and Rozanne's boyfriend, Tom, struck out Friday night.

Long before we approached the exit, cars had ground to a standstill and police were urging everyone to turn around and go home. Even more intrigued, we pulled our car over, slept a few hours, and then backtracked to a local grocery store and asked if there was a back way in. There was, and eventually, we squeezed the car into a tight spot and eagerly joined the cavalcade of pilgrims.

A Sea of Youth

Once inside the trampled gates, Roy and I separated from Rozanne and Tom (we don't remember why or how). For the next eighteen hours, Roy and I sat among a burgeoning group of strangers—a sea of youth. The smell of marijuana wafted through the air so thickly we experienced a contact high. Although I was afraid to accept the offered tokes, Roy gamely indulged. I was still a "good girl" who had not yet broken free of parental and

Photo on following page: Youths protest the Vietnam War at UCLA in 1972. Some people point to Woodstock as the start of their political activism. (Getty Images.)

societal strictures. Plus, an announcer kept spreading the word that this or that "acid is bad," and I worried that the marijuana cigarettes might have other drugs laced into the weed.

Despite this wariness, I felt oddly safe, immersed in my generation's culture, one with the swelling crowd, an amoeba in a far larger organism, symbiotic and minuscule. The music bonded us; our humanity engulfed us; our sense of global significance embodied and empowered us as a swaggering band of youthful dreamers. "The counterculture," as *they* called us, had a visual—400,000 yearning children, as one, portrayed credibility, voice, adrenaline, vision. Our longing for peace, for change, for brilliant futures for ourselves as individuals, and for the human race as one, beat as loudly as the thundering drums onstage.

> What I remember specifically is perching on an abandoned Maxwell House coffee can; sleeping curled into [the] fetal position on a piece of shared cardboard that slid around in the oozing mud.

What I Remember

What I remember specifically is perching on an abandoned Maxwell House coffee can; sleeping curled into [the] fetal position on a piece of shared cardboard that slid around in the oozing mud; the forcefulness of an omnipresent anti-war sentiment; the army helicopters circling overhead; and the dangerous paranoia and anger they generated. Was the government going to spy on us, threaten us, disband us, or gas us? I remember the cheers that arose when the announcer told us they were bringing us food, water, and medical supplies, and that someone on board had flashed a peace sign.

I remember the joyful, even jubilant, atmosphere that followed, crawling up a muddy hillside by grabbing outstretched hands, standing in long lines to use the foul-smelling portable toilets, being hungry, wet, tired, and thirsty. Through it all, I remember the music and how it bound us together. One after another, musicians and groups played the songs that we already loved or would grow to love. They were our anthem, our identity, and the demarcation line from that of our parents. These were our troubadours, the truth-tellers, the rebels we admired and emulated.

> Our country was in turmoil, but 400,000 contemporaries came together to celebrate life, music, and joy and had the phenomenal experience of realizing that we were one.

I remember walking through the chilled night air at 4 A.M., retracing our steps until we reached the car and crawled inside to sleep. I remember the trip home; our tongues wagging with tales; our recognition that we had all gone through something so extraordinary that going back to our everyday lives would not erase it. Our country was in turmoil, but 400,000 contemporaries came together to celebrate life, music, and joy and had the phenomenal experience of realizing that we were one. What I remember most is the sense that my generation could make a difference— that the world would soon become ours to ruin or to save.

Prior to Woodstock, I had attended peace demonstrations and often stood warily on the sidelines, watching others raise signs, make speeches, chant slogans, and taunt "the establishment," as *we* called them. After Woodstock, I moved more freely into the fray, even planted myself on the floor of a local university library during a "sit in," and told my mother I was spending the weekend at a friend's house when, in actuality—a short time after the Ohio National Guard murdered four students at Kent State—I piled into a Chevy Impala with seven other girls and rode to Washington, D.C., where I saw, for the first time in an up-close-and-personal way, soldiers lining the streets of Washington, their guns trained on us. Buoyed by the strength in our numbers and the memories of Woodstock, I gathered my generation's ideals to my heart and stood shoulder-to-shoulder with students shouting for an end to the Vietnam War.

I was never a hippie—not even close—unlike my sister who loved dirty, ratty jeans, I neatly pressed my bell-bottoms. But I was an idealistic dreamer who went on to become a reporter, a field in which ideals served me well. Rozanne and Roy—who was a hippie briefly—became teachers, molding young souls in important ways. For years afterward, we gleefully reminisced about Woodstock. But it wasn't until I was living in Paris in 2003 that I had another "Woodstock moment."

A Woodstock Moment in Paris

I had only been in Paris a few months and did not speak the language, but accompanied a Parisian friend to the anti-war demonstration leading up to the invasion of Iraq [in March 2003]. The air was electric, the mood jovial despite the reason we had gathered. As we waited for hours for the march to begin, new arrivals by the hundreds of thousands filled the street, tightening our personal space to a few inches. The lines of police multiplied, and feelings intensified until someone placed a huge speaker on the roof of his truck and blasted, *We Are Family* . . . and suddenly everyone sang and danced, as one, and I felt just as I had felt thirty-four years earlier, in a muddy field on Max Yasgur's farm.

> To this day, memories of Woodstock make me yearn for those heady days when the youth of America took up the sword.

To this day, memories of Woodstock make me yearn for those heady days when the youth of America took up the sword. Woodstock wasn't a dream, it happened . . . it affected the way many of us viewed the world and our place in it. The phenomenon of Woodstock created waves in world consciousness, and the seemingly boundless creativity that had taken root throughout the decade blossomed. For no less than that, it's worth remembering and honoring, and perhaps more importantly, because many young people today yearn for a similarly empowering experience. Oh, if we could rise again in solidarity and strength, we could once again transform the world.

A Woodstock Musician Recounts the Experience

David Crosby

In the following firsthand account, David Crosby, of the band Crosby, Stills, Nash, and Young, tells the story of the group's appearance at Woodstock. Crosby frankly explains that his memories are a little fuzzy because of the particularly powerful marijuana that he was smoking. His primary recollection is of the mud, but he also remembers walking through the crowd, and seeing hippies and police come together to help a young woman who had cut her foot. When it came time to perform, he and the other band members were scared, not because of the crowd but because the musicians they most respected were all watching from backstage. The group was trying a new sound, and the Woodstock performance was only the second time they had tried it. Their set was a big hit, and their appearance in the movie of the festival made them stars. David Crosby is an American musician and songwriter and a member of the Rock and Roll Hall of Fame.

SOURCE. Joel Makower, *Woodstock: The Oral History* [40th Anniversary Edition], Albany, NY: SUNY Press, 2009. Copyright © 2009 Joel Makower. Reproduced by permission of the State University of New York Press and the author.

We were just starting our first tour as Crosby, Stills, Nash, and Young. We had played the previous night in the Chicago Auditorium theater, two shows. That was our first show anywhere—ever—with Joni Mitchell opening. Joni wanted to come [to Woodstock] but was supposed to do "The Dick Cavett Show" the next night or the night after. And by the time we were ready to go here, her manager told her, "Hey, look, you can't go. You might not be able to get back out."

We hired a plane somewhere, probably Long Island, and flew out to where the helicopters were picking people up and taking them out to the site. I don't know where that was. I don't remember much about it. At the time I was high as a kite. We got in the helicopter and flew out to it and by this time I was realizing that it was way more than anybody had realized was going to happen.

We flew in. I think Nash told me that his helicopter lost its tail rudder and auto-rotated down the last twenty feet and scared him to death. I got in easy as pie and slogged through the mud. If there is an overriding impression of Woodstock, it's mud. There was a ton of mud everywhere, all the time. And after that it was a blur. I can remember flashes. I remember a tent. I remember that Christine, my girlfriend, was very unhappy that she had dressed up pretty to come because we were in a field of deep mud and a tent. At one point, I think I went to a motel. They got me to a motel. I'm not sure how they did that because the roads were impassable in all directions all the time.

Part of my haziness about it is due to the fact that this was when I first encountered a kind of pot that I've since come to call Pullover Pot. It was Colombian Gold, little tiny budlets of gold Colombian pot; it still had that fresh-turned dirt furrow smell. But if

> " At that point we were all thrilled with the idea that our values were triumphant someplace in the world. "

you smoked it—I remember smoking it for the first time in Florida, and I was driving someplace and I smoked it and I pulled over and listened to the radio for a while because I couldn't remember where I was going. And some friends of mine, a guy named Rocky and another guy named Big John, had brought a bunch of this stuff up and they were just giving it to their favorite people. And so I was in a ripe old state wandering around there. A lot of people were on psychedelics. I didn't take psychedelics to play; I couldn't. If you take it and try to play, the guitar gets three feet thick and the strings turn to rubber and it just doesn't work.

I remember images. I remember we didn't just stay backstage. I snuck out and I wandered around; nobody really knew who anybody was. I remember being out at dusk and seeing this state trooper carrying a little girl who had just cut her foot. A pretty little girl. She had stepped on a piece of glass in the mud and he was carrying her back to his car. He carried her back, put her in the seat, got something wrapped around her foot and it was soaked with blood. And I watched about the nearest twenty or thirty hippies push this police car out of the mud. And I thought to myself, "Hmmm, something other than the usual is going on here."

Because there was no animosity. There was a feeling going on with everybody at that point. We felt very encouraged by seeing each other. Everybody was thrilled that there were so many of us. We thought, "Hey, we're going to change everything. We're going to stop the war tomorrow." Well, it didn't work out that way. But at that point we were all thrilled with the idea that our values were triumphant someplace in the world. That, at least for this one small space of time in this one little town in New York, the hippie ethic was the ruling way to do. And it felt great. I can't say that it would have solved all the world's problems if it had spread and taken over everywhere. I don't even know if it would work. But I know

Photo on previous page: David Crosby played at both the 1969 and 1994 Woodstock festivals. **(Getty Images.)**

that for that weekend for that town in New York, it was great. It felt great. It felt wonderful. There wasn't any of the classic "I don't want to get involved." If somebody had a problem, you tried to help them. If you had a sandwich and somebody was hungry, you'd tear it in half. That was how everybody was doing it right then.

I remember being terrified playing. Stephen [Stills] said it when we were onstage, but we *were* scared. It wasn't that we were scared of playing in front of that many people because frankly you didn't know it was that many people. It was nighttime when we played, so we could only see the first forty or fifty rows of people. But also, your mind just doesn't count that high. Your mind goes, "One, two, three, many." Imagine for yourself half a million dots. How many is it, what space does it take? We were scared because everybody we thought was cool in the world that played music was standing around behind us in a row, all in a huge semi-circle behind the amps. Everybody. Everybody that we respected in the world was right there—the [Grateful] Dead, [Jefferson] Airplane, [Jimi] Hendrix, Sly [Stone], Country Joe [McDonald], and just a ton of people, you know, a ton. We were not intimidated but we knew we were on the line because we were the new boy in town. Everybody else knew how everybody else sounded. The first blush had been worn off of Hendrix lighting his guitar on fire and The Who kicking their drums apart. They had already seen that. I think a lot of it was just that we were so different from everybody else. It was the year of the guitar player. Everybody wanted to be [Eric] Clapton and Hendrix. And we came along singing three-part harmony and it was just great timing.

> We were scared because everybody we thought was cool in the world that played music was standing around behind us in a row, all in a huge semi-circle behind the amps.

But nobody had seen us get up and try to sing harmony together. This was *it*. This was *the* first time. The only time we'd done it, like I said, was the night before in Chicago. So they all came. Everybody came out of every crack and crevice and cranny and tent and mud hole in the area and they were all standing there on stage. Everybody that had a right to be on that stage under any circumstances at all was on it at the time. If it was going to collapse, that's when it would have collapsed. And, of course, we were nervous.

And we were good, thank God. It went down very well. Oh, they loved it, everybody loved it. How could you not love it? "Suite: Judy Blue Eyes"—what's not to like? They loved it because they're musicians and they knew that this was something new and something good so they all loved it. And the people who were my real close friends—Paul Kantner and Grace Slick, [Jerry] Garcia, and a lot of people—they were all thrilled. They said, "Wow! You tore it up!" It worked.

Since then, because we were in the movie [the Woodstock documentary] and because everybody knows who we are, I've been asked what Woodstock was like probably more than any other question except, "How did you guys meet?" So I've gotten very tired of talking about it. In general, [if] somebody asked me what was Woodstock like I tell them muddy. But it was, if you want to know, it was a thrill.

A French Visitor Recalls His Favorite Woodstock Moments

Francis Dumaurier

On his first trip to the United States, the author of the following selection had an unexpected Woodstock experience. Shortly after he and his friend arrived in New York City, they heard about Woodstock and along with four others crammed into a Mustang convertible for the drive to Bethel. Not wanting to miss this rare event, when the car became stuck in traffic, he and his friend walked the rest of the way to join "a sea of kindred spirits on another planet." He also relates his favorite musical moments. After the festival, while riding the subway covered in mud, they were proud of having been part of such a momentous event. Francis Dumaurier is an actor living in New York City. After Woodstock, he returned to France to finish his studies but soon returned and later became an American citizen.

SOURCE. Francis Dumaurier, *Woodstock Revisited*, edited by Susan Reynolds, Avon, MA: Adams Media, 2009. Copyright © 2009 by Susan Reynolds. Reproduced by permission.

August 10, 1969. I'm flying from Paris to JFK [John F. Kennedy airport in New York City] with my friend Loïc. We're excited about discovering the land of rock'n'roll. It's our first trip to the States and we're the first of our group of friends to cross the Atlantic. We land to refuel in Canada and, as we wait, a young guy asks us if we're going to Woodstock. This event is news to us, but we're instantly interested—after all, we've just seen *Monterey Pop* and *Easy Rider* in Parisian theaters to prepare for our great American adventure.

A Musical Adventure

Mark comes to pick us up at JFK to drive us to his cousin David's house, where we can stay until we take a bus to San Francisco. We met Mark and David when they visited Europe during the summer of 1967 and stayed in touch by mail.

Honky Tonk Women is the first song we hear on the radio on our way to Manhattan, where we walk to Central Park and, unbelievable but true, Jefferson Airplane is giving a free concert on the grass. The buzz is: next weekend—Woodstock. David offers to arrange for tickets and carpooling through a local FM radio station, if we're interested. Interested??? Like we have better things to do???

Back at David's house we listen to The Band's *Big Pink* and The Beach Boys' *20/20*; later, we visit his friends to hear The Who's *Tommy* in its entirety.

The Journey to Woodstock

We have tickets for Saturday and Sunday. We meet our hosts on Friday night and six of us cram in a white Mustang convertible. We sit like sardines, and we don't mind the drizzle as we ride on the New York State Thruway until we get stuck in traffic . . . literally . . . in the middle of the Thruway. So, Loïc, David, and I thank our gracious hosts and start walking through the fields toward a

> On my first weekend ever in America, I join a sea of kindred spirits on another planet. I know right away that I'm where I belong.

country road where traffic is slow but moving. We find a ride, sit in the car, and the rain starts pouring.

As we move like snails, we hear on the car radio that, because of the weather, the concert is canceled and the governor has officially declared the place a disaster area, asking one and all to return to where they came from. We look at each other and ponder what to do. I tell Loïc that, since I'm so close to the place, I have to see the stage even if the concert is canceled and the place closed.

Loïc decides to come with me on the long walk to Max Yasgur's farm. Luckily, the rain has stopped, and the sun is peeking through. Along the way, people are amazingly friendly, giving us biscuits and water.

We finally enter the arena. What an amazing site. On my first day in America, I get to see Jefferson Airplane in the park. Now, on my first weekend ever in America, I join a sea of kindred spirits on another planet. I know right away that I'm where I belong.

Favorite Moments

My favorite moments: Mountain's thunderous aural attack, Canned Heat's "Boogie" at night while small fires are burning on the hills, waking up to the unmistakable voice of Janis Joplin, falling asleep after The Who's complete performance of *Tommy*, awakening to the call of Grace Slick at the crack of dawn, Alvin Lee's false start and fiery version of "[I'm] Going Home," Carlos Santana's hot dance beat, CSN&Y's melodic but humble beginnings, John Sebastian's dreamy touch, Joe Cocker belting it out as the storm gathers strength, waking up to The Paul Butterfield Blues band's unscheduled performance, standing in disbelief in a field of wet muddy garbage as Jimi Hendrix plays a very long set to a much smaller crowd while a girl keeps screaming "'Voodoo Chile,' I want 'Voodoo Chile' " until he finally obliges. . . .

Proud Woodstock Veterans

The time has come to leave the site, and a state trooper asks us if we need a ride. He stops a car and asks the driver to drop us at the Monticello bus depot. In Manhattan, we take the C train to David's Upper West Side apartment. People on the subway are reading daily papers with headlines like "3 Days of Drugs, Sex, and Rock'n'Roll." We stand beaming, a little frazzled, covered with mud. People are watching us as if we are zombies.

In December, four months after Woodstock, I go to the Altamont speedway [in California] to see The Rolling Stones' free concert, which is already called "Woodstock West." It's a disaster, but I am happy to have come and witnessed in person how Woodstock came and went, and why it can never be duplicated.

When the artificial re-creation of Woodstock is planned in 1994, I contact all the media of New York City to speak against this fallacy. Nobody returns my calls, the event is a dud, and I hope it never happens again.

> There were no drugs and sex for me, but there was plenty of rock 'n roll.

I passed a masters degree in American studies at the University of Paris in 1971 and eventually became a proud American citizen twenty-five years ago. Woodstock is where my current life started and the original program of the event is framed, along with my very own concert and muddy emergency food tickets, on the wall facing me.

There were no drugs and sex for me, but there was plenty of rock 'n roll. The most important is that I was there and that I remember everything—a heck of a field trip!

A Photographer and His Subjects Recall An Iconic Woodstock Moment

Timothy Dumas

In the following article, a writer tells of people who, without knowing each other, crossed paths at the festival and became part of the Woodstock history. The embracing couple who appear on the cover of the Woodstock sound track album are Nick Ercoline and his girlfriend Bobbi Kelly. In the bar where Nick worked, the couple heard about the traffic jam to the festival and decided they wanted to be part of the momentous event. After arriving, they found a spot on a slope and joined the "sea of humanity." Photographer Burk Uzzle, who wanted to cover Woodstock his own way, was camping nearby with his family. On the morning of the final day, he wandered the outskirts of the festival when "magically this couple stood up and hugged." Uzzle took several photographs until the light was gone and "the mood was over." Timothy Dumas is an arts writer and the author of true crime books.

SOURCE. Timothy Dumas, "Still Together Now," *Smithsonian*, vol. 40, August 2009, pp. 6–8. Reproduced by permission of the author.

On August 15, 1969, Nick Ercoline was tending Dino's bar in Middletown, New York, while his girlfriend of ten weeks, Bobbi Kelly, sat on a stool, sipping nickel draft beer and listening to the news on the radio. In the past 30 days, Senator Ted Kennedy had driven off a bridge at Chappaquiddick Island, the Apollo 11 astronauts had planted a flag on the moon and the Charles Manson family had murdered eight Californians, including actress Sharon Tate, in Los Angeles. In the soft green hills of Catskills dairy country, such events seemed worlds away.

Two Woodstock Tales

That Friday night, however, waves of American youths were surging toward Max Yasgur's farm in Bethel, New York, 40 miles up the road, for three days of something called the Woodstock Music and Art Fair. A hush fell over Dino's as newscasters told of epic traffic jams and crowd estimates rising to 500,000. When they heard a rumor . . . that a glut of cars had shut down the New York State Thruway, the 20-year-old sweethearts could no longer resist. "We just got to thinking, we were never going to see anything like this the rest of our lives, ever," Nick says.

Earlier that same day, photographer Burk Uzzle, a *Life* magazine alumnus and a member of the elite Magnum photo agency, had driven upstate from Manhattan with his wife and two young sons to camp on the trout-filled Neversink River. Uzzle had declined an invitation from *Newsweek* to cover Woodstock, thinking he would just duck in and shoot it his way instead, then retreat to his campsite. "I really don't like to work on assignment, to tell you the truth," he says. "Because then I'm obligated to do what editors want me to do, and that's usually the wrong thing."

As Uzzle walked amid Woodstock's many potential disasters—rain, drugs, food and water shortages—he felt

Photographer Burk Uzzle shot an iconic image of festival attendees Nick Ercoline and Bobbi Kelly hugging. (Time & Life Pictures/Getty Images.)

something of an Aquarian spirit in the air. "I'd say to my colleagues down by the stage, 'Hey, you guys, it's incredible out there. The girls are taking their clothes off. The guys, too. It's really beautiful,'" he recalls. "And they'd tell me, 'No, no, no, the editor wants me to stay here and get Ravi Shankar.'"

On Saturday morning Nick and Bobbi, with friends Mike Duco, Cathy Wells and Jim "Corky" Corcoran, a Vietnam veteran fresh from the Marines, set off in Corcoran's mother's 1965 Impala station wagon down country lanes and across cow pastures. In standstill traffic a few miles from Bethel, they parked the Impala, flagged down a van full of naked hippies, then walked the final stretch to Yasgur's farm. A spaced-out Californian named Herbie tagged along, carrying a wooden staff with a plastic butterfly dancing from the tip. The group claimed a patch of mud on the rim of a slope. "It was a sea of humanity," Bobbi says. "Someone with a guitar here, someone making love there, someone smoking a joint, someone puking his brains out, the din of the music you could hear over all of this—a bombardment of the senses."

> 'Grace Slick of Jefferson Airplane was singing, bringing up the dawn. . . . And just magically this couple stood up and hugged.'

A Magical Moment

Early Sunday morning, Uzzle, happily stuck at Woodstock, left his makeshift tent with two Leicas [cameras] strapped round his neck. "Grace Slick of Jefferson Airplane was singing, bringing up the dawn," he remembers. "And just magically this couple stood up and hugged." They kissed, smiled at each other, and the woman leaned her head on the man's shoulder. "I just had time to get off a few frames of black and white and a few of color, then the light was over and the mood was over," Uzzle says of what would become his best-known photograph. His subjects never noticed.

One night in 1970, Corcoran brought the just-released Woodstock soundtrack album to Bobbi's apartment. The cover showed a vast hillside strewn with sleepy bodies and a couple locked in a tired, happy embrace. "That's Herbie's butterfly," Nick said, his eye going to the bright spot of color. Corcoran told him to look again. "Oh, hey! That's Bobbi and me!" (Over the years, several people have seen themselves as the couple on the album cover. Corcoran, cropped out of that image, appears in the full frame, lying in an Army blanket. "There is no doubt in my mind that it's me and Bobbi and Nick Ercoline," he says.)

Not a Counterculture Couple

After that first shock of recognition, the couple gave little thought to the photograph for nearly two decades, until *Life* tracked down Bobbi for a 20th-anniversary article in 1989. "After hearing our story," she says today, "I think some people are disappointed that we were not . . ."

". . . Full-fledged hippies," Nick says.

"That we were not out-and-out flower power and revolution. I was just a country girl. He was just a two-job college student." Married for 38 years with two grown sons, they now live in Pine Bush, 45 minutes southeast of Bethel. Bobbi is an elementary school nurse; Nick, a retired carpenter, is a building inspector for Orange County.

> 'We were not out-and-out flower power and revolution. I was just a country girl. He was just a two-job college student.'

Uzzle, 71 and living in his native North Carolina, is still making photographs. His work hangs in galleries and museums around the world. And his Woodstock photograph hangs, poster-size, above Nick and Bobbi's breakfast table.

"I look at it every day," Bobbi says. "I met Nick, we fell in love and it was the beginning of my best life." The embrace may have been theirs alone, but the image captures a romantic moment in America's collective memory. If that moment would soon seem overtaken by Altamont or Kent State or Cambodia, then Nick and Bobbi's marriage offers reassurance: the Woodstock moment was real, and it endures.

A Woodstock Festivalgoer Explains Why the Experience Cannot Be Reproduced

Pip Klein

In the following viewpoint, a woman compares her 1969 Woodstock experience to a commemorative concert she attended in 1998 at the Monticello Raceway, located near the original festival site. Unlike her experience at the original event, where she and her friends had to abandon their car and walk four miles to the site, the traffic to get to the 1998 concert was manageable and parking easy. The 1998 crowd was also much smaller than the nearly half million who attended the 1969 festival. While listening to the announcer, Klein also notes that the 1998 event reflects the ideals of an era more interested in making money than making love. Although the confluence of "cosmic forces" that made Woodstock a benchmark for a

SOURCE. Pip Klein, "You Can't Go Home Again: A Personal Journey from Woodstock Back to the Garden," *Hudson Valley Business Journal*, vol. 9, August 31–September 7, 1998, p. 32. Reproduced by permission of the author.

generation cannot be duplicated, she concludes that it is still fun to reminisce. *Pip Klein is associate publisher of the* Hudson Valley Business Journal.

"You were there? You went to Woodstock?" When people hear my "yes" response, their voices take on a certain reverential awe, a respect that is perhaps unwarranted. All I did was happen to be camping out in Max Yasgur's field one hot, rainy, muddy weekend—August 15–17, 1969. Of course, there were 400,000 other people with me on those 600 acres. And we were listening to some of the best rock music of the time (any time!). But what's so great about that? I ask. "You were at the source," the awestruck will say. "You were part of IT!"

A Benchmark Moment

"It" was officially called "the Woodstock Music and Art Fair: An Aquarian Exposition." And the people who did go, didn't go expecting what Woodstock would come to stand for—a benchmark for a generation. We had come just to hear the music, but left with something else—the experience of copyrighting a new nation!

"Some monstrous and marvelous metaphor had come alive, revealing itself in terms of its contradictions: sharing and profiteering, sky and mud, love and death," wrote Andrew Kopkind in *Currents* later that year. And for those who were there, it will always be like the memory of an eclipse: as you are standing there watching it, you know that it's an incredible coming together of cosmic forces—and it's never going to happen again.

Fast Forward

But that doesn't stop us from trying! Fast forward to Saturday, August 15, 1998, where I'm picking up tickets for "A Day in the Garden at the Monticello Raceway.

THE FESTIVAL EXPERIENCE THEN AND NOW	
1969	**1998**
lawn	lawn chairs
strolling	strollers
sunburn	sunscreen
Yasgur's farm	Yasgur's ice cream
Nothing to drink	iced cappuccino
Richie Havens	Richie Havens
It was a happening.	It happened.

Taken from: Pip Klein, "You Can't Go Home Again: A Personal Journey from Woodstock Back to the Garden," *Hudson Valley Business Journal*, August 31–September 7, 1998.

"Do you know how to get there?" asks the pleasant young woman inside the booth. "Haven't been there in 29 years," I laughed, "But I think I'll be able to find it."

And not only did I find it—getting there was a breeze. A manageable stream of traffic followed orderly rows of bright orange cones that had made [Route] 17B into three lanes. Friendly yellow-shirted staffers pointed the way, personally ushering our car into a neat space a short walk away from the site. This is more like it, I thought, remembering how our group of Orange County locals (newly minted high school grads) had cleverly (inadvertently) thought to drive up a back road via Port Jervis only to have to abandon the car four miles from the site when we realized that traffic was totally frozen.

But today, my husband, three-year old son and merry band of friends and I pushed our stroller up to Sullivan County's most famous field. And this time, tickets were really taken at the gates. As we emerged onto the rim of the wonderful natural amphitheater, I felt my spine tingle at the memory of it all. The sea (albeit smaller) of people, and the way the sky fits over the field like a perfect dome, same kind of dark clouds threatening, but cooling us as we descended the hill.

We threw out a spacious blanket for our little group to set up camp (the same area probably had been home to hundreds!) and sat back to enjoy the music, explore the grounds and—well, go shopping!

Under sharply-peaked white tents, looking like Denver's new airport, was everything imaginable from the expected tie-die tee shirts (I paid $25 for a kid size!), to pantyhose (I'm not kidding!). Not to mention a variety of foods that rivals any restaurant row in Manhattan (Thai, Chinese, Italian, Greek etc.!).

Flashback

In between sets, WDST radio's Dave Leonard took the mike to make some announcements. I flashed back to my own '69 favorite (No, not the one about the bad acid)—this one: "We've just been declared the third largest city in the State of New York!" I was trying to figure out the numerical size of the crowd (turned out to be 20,000) and where we'd rank in an urban pecking order this time, when my 'New York State of Mind' reverie was interrupted by Leonard's booming voice: "Don't worry if you run out of money," he bellowed from the stage. "Because there's an ATM up there."

> If someone shouted out 'I'm hungry' back then, they would have been pelted with oranges or whatever anyone wanted to share—but this wasn't make love—this was the 90s: make money!

I laughed at myself, because for one naive nostalgic second I had really thought he was going to say: "Don't worry—if you run out of money—we're giving away free food!" If someone shouted out "I'm hungry" back then, they would have been pelted with oranges or whatever anyone wanted to share—but this wasn't make love—this was the 90s: make money!

But, hey, at least we were all on the hallowed ground of the original Woodstock site and the music was good (I hung on every word of Joni Mitchell's set, especially a sultry "Summertime" and her encore must-sing original "Woodstock").

> Even though you can't go home again, it is certainly fun trying to get back to that garden.

And when and if they try to stage our 30th celebration next year, I'm hoping that I'll get to hear Santana's hypnotizing congas echoing off the Catskills. Because you can dream, and even though you can't go home again, it is certainly fun trying to get back to that garden.

In 1979, as promoters were attempting to stage "Woodstock II," a "ten years after" reunion, spokesperson Tom Falter summed up the 1969 event: "A spiritual Woodstock is what it was. God put on the first one and that's a hard act to follow."

CHRONOLOGY

1966   John Roberts, with a multimillion-dollar trust fund, and Joel Rosenman, a recent Yale Law School graduate, meet on a golf course, and by 1967 share an apartment in Manhattan, New York.

1968   March: Roberts and Rosenman place an ad in the *Wall Street Journal* and the *New York Times* that reads, "Young Men with Unlimited Capital looking for interesting, legitimate investment opportunities and business propositions."

October: Festival promoter and rock-group manager Michael Lang, hoping to sign a record deal for his band, meets with Artie Kornfeld, a songwriter and vice president of Capitol Records. Shortly after this meeting, Lang moves into the New York City apartment of Kornfeld and his wife. There they discuss plans about hosting a rock concert and opening a recording studio in Woodstock, New York, a mecca for the rock musicians and other artists of the day.

1969   February: Lang and Kornfeld meet with Roberts and Rosenman to discuss plans for a festival to generate funds for the recording studio. Shortly thereafter, the four young men form Woodstock Ventures.

March: Woodstock Ventures leases the 300-acre Mills Industrial Park in Wallkill, New York, for $10,000. Lang begins to sign acts and radio stations being to talk about the upcoming festival.

April: Ads for the festival run in the *Village Voice* and *Rolling Stone* magazine. Festival advertising runs primarily on FM radio stations and in underground newspapers.

May: Ads run in the *New York Times*. When ads run in the *Times Herald-Record*, a local newspaper near the festival site, local opposition begins to grow. Residents fear that the promoters were misleading them. Indeed, promoters had said that only 50,000 people would attend a "folk" festival, when they actually expected as many as 250,000 at a "rock" concert.

June: Woodstock Ventures hires Wes Pomeroy to head security. He plans to use off-duty police officers who will not wear uniforms or carry guns.

Preparation of the industrial site begins and Woodstock Ventures staff attend Wallkill board meetings to allay fears.

Counterculture activists, including Abbie Hoffman, claim Woodstock Ventures is only interested in making money off the people in the counterculture movement.

Woodstock Ventures hires the Hog Farm, an entertainment/activist commune in New Mexico, to clear trails, build a playground for children, and prepare the campgrounds. The Hog Farm would later run "trip tents" to help people on bad LSD trips, and founding member Hugh Romney, also known as comic Wavy Gravy, would serve as occasional festival emcee.

June 27: The *Times Herald-Record* reports that the city of Wallkill "has declared war on the proposed rock-folk festival."

July 15: The Wallkill Zoning Board bans the festival in a four-page decision.

Shortly after reading about the ban, Elliot Tiber of White Lake, New York, invites Woodstock Ventures to use his hotel for the festival. Lang does not think the location will work.

July 18: Local farmer Max Yasgur leases his land to festival promoters for $50,000. (An additional $75,000 is put in escrow to cover damages.)

July 20: Neil Armstrong walks on the moon.

July 21: Bethel approves the festival. The same day, trucks arrive with building materials and preparation begins in earnest, but rain plagues progress.

July 25: Woodstock Ventures runs ads for five days depicting Wallkill residents who opposed the festival as hillbillies to stoke the controversy and create publicity to stimulate ticket sales.

July 29: Liberty, New York, ten miles from the festival site, measures 4.33 inches of rain, the most ever recorded there on a single day in July.

August 7: Hog Farm members arrive at JFK airport in New York City. Comic Hugh Romney jokes with reporters who ask if they are providing security.

August 11: People begin to filter into the festival site, but the campgrounds are not yet ready.

August 13: The New York City police department forbids off-duty police officers from working at the festival without wearing a uniform, shield, or gun, which effectively prevents those officers who had agreed to help with security from overtly doing so.

The head of the New York State troopers refuses to implement a traffic plan.

Local residents plan to form a human barricade across Route 17B, but on the day of the planned barricade, the route is already jammed for ten miles.

August 14: Artie Kornfeld makes a deal with Warner Brothers to make a film of the festival.

New York State police officers using fake names show up to help with festival security, asking to be paid double and in cash. Needing security, Woodstock Ventures reluctantly agrees, calling it extortion.

Approximately 25,000 people arrive, but ticket booths have not been erected.

August 15: At least 200,000 people fill the festival field.

Michael Wadleigh signs on to direct filming of the festival for a documentary.

At around 8 A.M., it begins to rain.

In the early afternoon, without ticket booths, it is clear that tickets will not be collected. An announcement is made from the stage, "The concert is free from now on."

In the late afternoon, security chief Wes Pomeroy makes an announcement for local radio stations, asking people not to travel to the festival as attendance has reached capacity.

At 5:07 P.M., after the rain has cleared, Richie Havens starts the festival while helicopters fly artists to the site because they are unable to get there by car due to the traffic.

Joan Baez concludes the first day of the festival with "We Shall Overcome" at around 2 A.M.

August 16: An announcement from the stage asks the audience to clean up their areas, and staff walk through with trash bags.

Seventeen-year-old Raymond Mizsak is fatally run over by a tractor while he sleeps.

Concerned about being paid for performing in a now free concert, managers for the Who, Janis Joplin, and the Grateful Dead demand payment in cash in advance. Charlie Prince, manager of the White Lake Bank, shuttled by helicopter, obtains cashier's checks to pay them.

National Guard helicopters transport donated food. Workers form a landing circle in a field to direct the helicopter and then transport the food to the free kitchens.

The weather begins to clear and Quill opens the show a little after noon.

Jefferson Airplane plays its set as the sun rises on August 17.

August 17: Two more attendees die: one from a heroin overdose, the other from a burst appendix. Despite claims that babies were born at the festival, the truth is that one was born in a car stuck in traffic and another at a local hospital after being airlifted by a helicopter.

Hugh Romney, aka Wavy Gravy, announces to the festival audience, "What we have in mind is breakfast in bed for four hundred thousand." The Hog Farm distributes cups of granola to the crowd.

Max Yasgur tells the audience, "This is the largest group of people ever assembled in one place, but I think you people have proven something to the world . . . that half a million young people can get together and have three days of fun and music—and have nothing but fun and music, and I God Bless You for it."

Rain and intermittent electricity outages interrupt performers throughout the day.

August 18: At 8:30 A.M., before about 40,000 remaining festivalgoers, Jimi Hendrix performs "The Star-Spangled Banner" in what some critics claim is a critique of the Vietnam War. In his guitar work he appears to imitate the fire of guns, the dropping of bombs, and flying rockets.

The festival ends with Hendrix's "Hey Joe" at 10:30 A.M.

The *New York Times* rock critic Mike Jahn and writer Barnard L. Collier, who were at the festival, make generally positive reports of the festival.

A *New York Times* editorial "Nightmare in the Catskills" makes disparaging remarks about the festival, saying, "What kind of culture is it that can produce so colossal a mess?" *Times* reporters actually at the festival are furious and threaten to quit. By the next day, the newspaper reflects a more positive view of the event because of pressure from reporters who actually attended the festival.

Late August: People begin filing lawsuits against Woodstock Ventures. In the end, about eighty lawsuits are filed.

Woodstock Ventures members discuss its dissolution when it is calculated that the partnership is $1.4 million in debt.

September 8: The *New York Times* reports that Lang and Kornfeld leave the partnership. Their buyout settlement is $31,750 each.

Warner Brothers pays $1 million to Rosenman and Roberts to buy out Woodstock Ventures' half of the film rights. Warner Brothers makes more than $50 million dollars on the film when it is released in March 1970.

October: The New York Health Department lists 797 documented instances of drug abuse at the festival.

1970   Woodstock Ventures refunds tickets bought by 12,000 to 18,000 people unable to reach the festival due to closed roads.

March 26: *Woodstock*, the documentary film, is released.

1971   The film of the festival is nominated for several Academy Awards, including film editing and sound. It wins the Oscar for best feature documentary.

1973   February 8: Max Yasgur dies.

1979   Several Woodstock musicians—Richie Havens, Country Joe and the Fish, Canned Heat, Rick Danko, and Paul Butterfield—gather at Madison Square Garden in a tenth anniversary event.

1981   Louis Nicky buys 37.5 acres, including the festival site, from the Yasgur estate. He dies five days before the twentieth anniversary of the festival, leaving the land to his companion, June Gelish.

1984   Wayne Saward, a Bloomingburg, New York, welder, builds a 5.5-ton cast iron and concrete monument to the festival.

1989   August 14–16: A spontaneous reunion attracts about 200,000 attendees.

1992   June Gelish and the town of Bethel prevent a gathering on the site by parking snowplows on surrounding roads.

1993   August: Plans for the twenty-fifth anniversary begin. Bethel approves a concert by Woodstock Ventures, but the plan is later rejected due to the proposed size of the crowd—250,000. Woodstock Ventures shifts its plans to a concert in Saugerties, New York.

Robert Gersh plans a 1994 concert in Bethel as does Sid Bernstein.

1994   January: Bethel approves Bernstein's plan. By July, however, only a few tickets to the event are sold.

August 13–14: Woodstock '94 is held in Saugerties, New York.

1996   The Library of Congress chooses *Woodstock* for preservation in the US National Film Registry as being "culturally, historically, or aesthetically significant."

Alan Gerry pays $1 million to June Gelish for approximately 1,400 acres in Bethel, including the festival site.

1998   August 14–16: Gerry produces a "Day in the Garden" at the original Woodstock site.

1999   July 23–25: Woodstock '99 is held at Griffiths Air Force Base in Rome, New York, with an estimated attendance of 225,000. Some attendees loot and set fires, rapes are reported, and seven people are injured.

August 15: A concert is held at Yasgur's farm on the thirty anniversary, featuring artists who performed at the original festival.

2000   May: New York state officials confirm that the Gerry Foundation is seeking state funding to build a museum and performing arts center at the Bethel site. State aid of $15 million is awarded in August.

2006   July 1: The New York Philharmonic plays the inaugural show at the new Bethel Woods Center for the Arts.

2008   June: The Museum at Bethel Woods opens.

2009   Instead of producing concerts, Artie Kornfeld, Michael Lang, and others publish books in the year of the festival's fortieth anniversary. Also released are fortieth anniversary editions of the movie and the sound track.

Country Joe McDonald hosts a concert tour, "Woodstock Heroes," at various venues nationwide, including Bethel on August 15.

August 26: Director Ang Lee's *Taking Woodstock*, a comedy film based on behind-the-scenes events, opens in theaters.

FOR FURTHER READING

Books

Andy Bennet, ed., *Remembering Woodstock*. Burlington, VT: Ashgate, 2004.

Anthony M. Casale and Philip Lerman, *Where Have All the Flowers Gone?: The Fall and Rise of the Woodstock Generation*. Kansas City, MO: Andrews McMeel, 1989.

Mike Evans and Paul Kingsbury, eds., *Woodstock: Three Days that Rocked the World*. New York: Sterling, 2009.

Klaus P. Fischer, *America in White, Black, and Gray: The Stormy 1960s*. New York: Continuum International, 2006.

Michael W. Flamm, *Debating the 1960s: Liberal, Conservative, and Radical Perspectives*. Lanham, MD: Rowman & Littlefield, 2008.

Ken Goffman and Dan Joy, *Counterculture Through the Ages: From Abraham to Acid House*. New York: Villard, 2004.

Sandra Gurvis, *Where Have All the Flower Children Gone?* Jackson: University Press of Mississippi, 2006.

Jerry Hopkins, *Festival! The Book of American Music Celebrations*. New York: Macmillan, 1970.

Rob Kirkpatrick, *1969: The Year Everything Changed*. New York: Skyhorse, 2009.

Artie Kornfeld, *The Pied Piper of Woodstock*. Delray Beach, FL: Spirit of the Woodstock Nation, 2009.

Michael Lang, *Woodstock Experience*. Columbus, MS: Genesis, 2009.

Brad Littleproud and Joanne Hague, *Woodstock: Peace, Music & Memories: 40th Anniversary*. Iola, WI: Krause, 2009.

Timothy Miller, *The Hippies and American Values*. Knoxville: University of Tennessee Press, 1991.

1969: Woodstock, the Moon and Manson: The Turbulent End of the '60s. New York: Time Inc., 2009.

Joel Rosenman, *Young Men with Unlimited Capital: The Story of Woodstock*. Houston: Scrivenery, 1999.

Robert Stephen Spitz, *Barefoot in Babylon: The Creation of the Woodstock Music Festival*. New York: Viking, 1979.

Rex Weiner and Deanne Stillman, *Woodstock Census: The Nationwide Survey of the Sixties Generation*. New York: Viking, 1979.

Jean Young and Michael Lang, *Woodstock Festival Remembered*. New York: Ballantine, 1979.

Periodicals

Billboard, "Three Days of Music, Mud & Myth: A Woodstock 1994 Survivor's Diary," August 27, 1994.

Christian Science Monitor, "Forty Years Later, What Part of Woodstock Lives On?," August 13, 2009.

Barnard L. Collier, "200,000 Thronging to Rock Festival Jam Roads Upstate," *New York Times*, August 16, 1969.

Economist, "Woodstock Rocked," August 30, 1969.

Christopher John Farley, "Woodstock Suburb," *Time*, August 22, 1994.

Larry Flick, Carla Hay, Melinda Newman, and Chris Morris, "In Woodstock's Wake, Hard Questions," *Billboard*, August 14, 1999.

Lacey Fosburgh, "346 Policemen Quit Music Festival," *New York Times*, August 15, 1969.

David Gates, "Twenty-five Years Later, We're Still Living in Woodstock Nation," *Newsweek*, August 8, 1994.

Tom Gogola, "Muckstock (Twenty-fifth Anniversary of the 1969 Woodstock Festival)," *Nation*, September 5, 1994.

Mark Guarino, "Did Woodstock Hippies Lead to US Financial Collapse?, *Christian Science Monitor*, February 25, 2010.

Doug Hall, "A Weekend Trip," *Women's Wear Daily*, August 18, 1969.

Philip Kopper, "Flashback to Woodstock," *American Heritage*, Summer 2009.

Patrick Lydon, "A Joyful Confirmation that Good Things Can Happen Here," *New York Times*, August 24, 1969.

William Murchison, "The Worst Years of Our Lives," *American Spectator*, October 2009.

New York Times, "Bethel Pilgrims Smoke 'Grass' and Some Take LSD to 'Groove,'" August 18, 1969.

New York Times, "Woodstock: Like It Was," August 25, 1969.

Michael Norman, "The 'Holy Ground' of the Woodstock Generation," *New York Times*, August 16, 1984.

Jon Pareles, "Back to the Garden, Without the Shock, or All That Mud," *New York Times*, August 16, 2009.

Jon Pareles, "Woodstock: A Moment of Muddy Grace," *New York Times*, August 9, 2009.

Richard Reeves, "Fair's Financier Calls It 'Success,' But He Estimates Losses as High as $2 Million," *New York Times*, August 18, 1969.

Valerie Seckler, "Woodstock Inc.," *Women's Wear Daily*, August 12, 2009.

Josh Simon and Gregory Heisler, "Back to the Garden," *Life*, August 1994.

Clifford Terry, "Mud, Music and . . . Middle Age: A Fond Look at the Last Great Freebie of the Western World," *Chicago Tribune*, July 30, 1989.

Josh Tyrangiel, "Taking Stock," *Time*, August 24, 2009.

Ray Waddell, "Peace and Prosperity," *Billboard*, August 8, 2009.

Websites

New York Times (http://topics.nytimes.com/top/reference /timestopics/subjects/w/woodstock_music_festivals/index .html). "Woodstock Music Festivals" is a section of the *New York Times* website with links to current and archived articles on the 1969 and later Woodstock festivals. Also included are slide shows, videos, and interactive media about the festivals.

Public Broadcasting System—Sunday Arts: Woodstock's 40th Anniversary (http://watch.thirteen.org/video/1210637104). An eleven-minute PBS *Sunday Watch* video that discusses the festival, its cultural relevance, and previews what visitors will find at the Museum at Bethel Woods, which memorializes the 1969 festival. The video includes music and film clips from the festival.

Woodstock Preservation Alliance: The Woodstock Preservation Archives (www.woodstockpreservation.org). The alliance website is dedicated to the historic preservation of the site of the 1969 Woodstock music festival. On the website are links to articles and essays, including firsthand accounts, pictures, and reports on the preservation of the festival site.

INDEX

A

Abraham, Morris, 51–52

Abruzzi, William, 145

Acid, *See* LSD, Drugs

ACORN (Assn. of Community Organizations for Reform Now), 115, 119, 120

Activist movements
anti-war (peace) movement, 94, 114, 137, 181–182
civil rights, 33, 35–37, 141, 156
Gay and Lesbian liberation, 33, 136, 141
green movement, 94, *95*, 97, 155
Women's Liberation, 141
See also Counterculture movement

Advertising, 116, 159–166, *173*

Aerosmith, 26, 174

Age of Aquarius, 22, 24

Agnew, Spiro, 105

Agri, Ticia Bernuth, 50

Alinsky, Saul, 114, 120

Altamont (Rolling Stones concert), 24–25, 98, 135, 137n1, 193, 198

Amatucci, Daniel, 55–57

Anderson, Ferdinand, 175

Antifashion movement, 82–83

Apollo 11, 98, 195

Aquarian Exposition. *See* Woodstock Music and Art Fair

Aquarium Drunkard (blog), 157

Areas, Jose, 142

Armstrong, Neil, 56, 98, 114

Aspen, Hal, 22, 27

Association of Chiefs of Police, 31

B

Baby boomers, 22–23, 113, 141, 152, 163

Baez, Joan, 18t, 25–26, 74–75, 91, 96, 103

The Band, 16, 28t, 93, 144, 162

Band of Gypsies, 70

Battle of Agincourt, 137, 137n2

Beatles, 25, 27, 62, 103

Benedict, Salli, 113, 118, 119

Berlin Wall, 124

Bernstein, Jacob, 122–128

Bestival, 97

Bethel Woods Center for the Arts, 127, 129, *131*, 153, 162

Big Pink medical tent, 17, 63

Black Panthers, 33

Blight, David, 130–132

Blood, Sweat and Tears, 28t, 76, 103

Blumer, Lee, 30–44

Boston Tea Party, 149

Boy Scouts, 23

Breslin, Jimmy, 34

Brown, Dave, 142

C

Calley, William, 98

Cambodia, 137, 198

Camille (hurricane), 76

Camp Winnarainbow, 116

Canned Heat, 23t, 192

Capitol Records, 16

Carabello, Mike, 142

Cateforis, Theo, 164–165

Chicago Seven Trial, 18

Christgau, Robert, 165

Christians for Social Action, 42

Civil Defense, 92

Civil rights movement, 33, 35–37, 141, 156

Civil War, 130, 132

Clapton, Eric, 188

Clark, Ben, 31

Clark, Ramsey, 36–37

Cocaine, 108, 145

Cocker, Joe, 25–26, 28t, 76, 96, 103, 192

Colbert, Stephen, 127

Collier, Barnard L., 86–93, 122, 124, 127, 134

Conscientious objectors, 177, 178

Cooke, Alistair, 67–71

Cooke, Douglas, 15–19

Corcoran, Jim "Corky," 196–197

Counterculture movement
advertising brands, 160
hippie communes, 17
media attitudes, 8
music and, 180
public opinion, 7
Woodstock mythology and, 4–5, 138, 140
Woodstock Ventures and, 17–19
See also Activist movements

Country Joe and the Fish, 28t, See also McDonald

Cranberries, 26

Creedence Clearwater Revival, 23t, 71, 103, 156

Creem (magazine), 157

Crosby, David, 184–189, 186

Crosby, Stills and Nash (CSN), 26–27, 93, 135

Crosby, Stills, Nash and Young (CSN&Y), 28t, 29, 103, 184–185, 192

Cummings, Bill, 113–114, 117–119

Currents (magazine), 200

Curry, Jack, 108

D

Dalton, David, 99–100

Dalton, Stephen, 94–101

Daltrey, Roger, 96

Death threats, 133

Deaths, 28–29, 90, 106, 126

DeCurtis, Anthony, 160

Déja Vu (Crosby, Stills, Nash, and Young), 29

Democratic National Convention of 1968
fear of riots at Woodstock and, 67
Hoffman and, 18
photograph, 35
Pomeroy and, 17
protest movement growth and, 58, 66n1
public reaction, 7, 68
violence, 4, 7, 66n1, 141

Dick Cavett Show, 162, 185

Dictionary of Cultural Literacy, 140

Donovan, 62

Doyle, Michael William, 138–150

Drugs
aftereffects, 108
arrests, 68, 93, 105
bad (drug) trip shelter, 17

bad reactions, 63, 64, 92, 145

cocaine, 108, 145

hashish, 64

heroin overdose, 28–29, 63, 68

LSD, 15, 62–64, 88–89, 92, 99–100

marijuana, 93, 105, 178, 184–187

media and, 84

peyote, 62

performers and, 99

personal stories, 184–187

pharmacy district, 20

psilocybin, 62

psychedelic (mind–altering) drugs, 4, 15, 62, 64, 88–89, 187

tolerance by law enforcement, 58

See also Medical care

Duco, Mike, 196

Dumas, Timothy, 194–198

Dumaurier, Francis, 190–193

Dylan, Bob, 16, 26, 65, 70, 103, 119, 144, 162, 175

E

Easy Rider (movie), 163

Eavis, Michael, 100

El Monaco Motel, 51

Elliott, Stuart, 163–164

Entertainment Weekly, 135–136

Ercoline, Nick, 195–198

Etheridge, Melissa, 174

F

Fabbri, John, 31, 42

Falter, Tom, 203

Farrell, Perry, 156–157

Fillmore concert halls, 25, 41, 149

Flower power, 26, 160, 198

Flower children, 62, 82, 96, 135, 137

Fogerty, John, 156

Food

concession booths, 17, 47

donations, 23, 180

food kitchen, 15

mismanagement, 59

shortages, 4, 15, 22, 87, 91–92, 106, 140, 147

Food for Love, 17, 19

Fornatale, Pete, 4–5

Foschiono, Louis, 60

Frankly Dankly bus, 112–113, 117, 120

G

Gabriel, Peter, 173

Gage, Justin, 157

Ganoung, Don, 31, 42, 47, 56, 57n2

Garbage, 68, 70, 92, 106, 192

Garcia, Jerry, 99, 189

Gay and Lesbian liberation, 33, 136, 141

Gehr, Richard, 165

General Mills, 164

Generation gap, 146

Girl Scouts, 23

Glastonbury music festival, 97, 100

Goldecker, Donald, 88–89

Goldstein, Stanley, 30–44, 47, 50–56, 57n2

Graham, Bill, 31, 41, 98, 142, 149

Grammy Awards, *161*

Grateful Dead, 19, 23t, 25, 62, 103, 124, 143, 188

Great Society programs, 113

Green Day, 26

Green movement, 94, *95,* 97, 155

Gregory, Dick, 36

Guthrie, Arlo, 18t, 28, 103, 125

H

Haight-Ashbury Diggers, 143
Hallock, Robin "Blue," *155*
Hardin, Tim, 16, 18t, 152
Hare Krishna, 65–66
Hashish, 64
Havens, Richie, 18t, 28, 118
Hell's Angels, 135, 137n1
Hendrix, Jimi
    acid rock and, 62
    bands, 70
    billing, 93
    biography, 70
    Crosby and, 188
    death, 25
    final act at Woodstock, 5, 28t, 132
    Monterey Pop Festival and, 143
    popularity, 74, 103, 124, 192–193
    Star Spangled Banner and, 65, 118
    Woodstock album and, 96
    Woodstock performance payment, 16
"Heroes of Woodstock" tour, 162
Hippies
    activism and, 33
    arrests, 19
    commercialism and, 24, 27, 156
    criticism, 103
    fashion, 82–83
    hippie ethic, 187–188
    media and, 7, 8
    photographs, *104*, *161*, *176*
    stereotypes, 109–110
    Woodstock and, 19–23, 58–66
    Max Yasgur and, 6
Hoffman, Abbie
    activist base at Woodstock, 136–137
    commercialism, 156

Democratic National Convention and, 18
flag shirt, 37
security at Woodstock and, 89, 104, 135
suicide, 108
Townshend and, 27, 105
writings, 23
yippies and, 44n1
Hog Farm Commune
current status, 116
drug problems and, 17, 64
free kitchen, 17
illegal activities, 18
security at Woodstock and, 89, 104, 135
Hoover, J. Edgar, 105
Hopper, Dennis, 163

I

Insecticide, 104
Iraq War, 160, 182
Iron Butterfly, 62, 162
Isserman, Maurice, 129–137

J

Jackson, Michael, 157
Jackson State University, 137
Jacques, Amy, 159–166
JazzTimes (magazine), 165
Jefferson Airplane, 23t, 62, 93, 103, 156, 188, 191
Jefferson Starship, 156
Jimi Hendrix Experience, 62, 70
Johnson, Lyndon B., 37, 111, 113, 150n1
Joplin, Janis
    death, 108
    Monterey Pop Festival and, 143
    performance at Woodstock, 23t, 25

popularity, 74, 93, 103
Woodstock documentary and, 96

K

Kantner, Paul, 156, 189
The Keef Hartley Band, 23t
Kelly, Bobbi, 195–198
Kennedy, Robert, 22, 34
Kennedy, Ted, 195
Kent State University, 25, 137, 181, 198
Kerner Commission, 141
Kerner, Otto, 150n1
King, Martin Luther Jr., 22, 136, 141
Kinnell, Chris, 114, 119
Kitchen, John, 119
Kopkind, Andrew, 200
Kornfeld, Artie, 6–7, 16, 39, 144
Kramer, Eddie, 98–100
Kramer, Lawrence, 122, 124
Kreis, Joe, 155
Kreis, Robert, 155
Kurosawa, Akira, 5

L

LaBianca, Rosemary, 98
Ladies of the Canyon (Mitchell), 29
Lang, Michael
    activist movements at Woodstock and, 136–137
    anniversary concerts and, 154–155
    entrance fees and, 6–7
    festival move to Yasgur Farm, 45–57
    green movement and, 94, 97, 155
    medical care and, 88
    Miami Pop Festival and, 16, 144
    Obama and, 101
    security and, 30–44

Woodstock Ventures and, 16
    writings, 97, 161
Laure, Jason, 167–170
Law Enforcement Assistance Administration, 37
Lawrence, Mel, 47, 50–51, 56, 57n2
Lawrence, Wade, 127–128, 153
Lawsuits, 28
Led Zeppelin, 39, 62
Lee, Alvin, 192
Lee, Ang, 135–136, 154, 161
Lee, Lawrence, 84
Lennon, John, 27, 162
Leonard, Dave, 202
Lerner, Steve, 58–66
Lieberman, Paul, 111–121
Life (magazine), 107–109, 122, 124, 195, 198
Lollapalooza, 157
Lovin' Spoonful, 143
LSD, 15, 62–64, 88–89, 92, 99–100
Luvs diapers, 163

M

Magic Mountain Festival, 143
Mailer, Norman, 34
Make Yourself Useful: Your Guide to the 21st Century (Schwerdtfeger), 160
Makower, Joel, 30–44
Mamas and the Papas, 143
Manson, Charles, 98, 195
Marcus, Greil, 125, 127
Marijuana, 93, 105, 178, 184–187
Marsh, Dave, 157
MASS MoCA, 121
McCain, John, 119

McCormick, Cody, 154
McDonald, Country Joe
    anti-war/peace stance, 94, 118, 130
    criticism of chant, 105
    Crosby and, 188
    crowd at Woodstock and, 97
    legacy of Woodstock and, 101
    Woodstock music lineup and, 18t, 28t
Media
    British media, 67–71
    conflicting reports on Woodstock, 58
    counterculture and, 7–8
    criticism of Woodstock, 79–85, 126–
        127, 134
    hippies and, 7, 8
    mythology of Woodstock and, 122
    nostalgia and, 163–164
    Obama inauguration and, 101
    praise for Woodstock, 9
    rock music as dangerous, 79–85
    traffic problem reportage, 125
    weather reporting, 75
    Woodstock sequels and, 107, 108, 154
    Max Yasgur and, 5
Medical care
    Big Pink medical tent, 17, 63
    Lang and, 88
    number of people treated, 145
    photograph, 90
    shortages, 87
    Woodstock sequels and, 145, 174–175
    See also Drugs
Meese, Ed, 154
Melanie, 18t, 28, 99, 101
Memorabilia, 161–163, 165
Mescaline, 64
Metallica, 174–175
Mexico, 142
Military draft, 98, 153, 160

Mindblender, 173
Mitchell, Artie, 54
Mitchell, Joni, 29, 154, 162, 185, 203
Mitchell, Joyce, 54
Mods, 82
Monterey Pop Festival, 19, 22, 70, 143, 148
Monterey Pop (movie), 70
Morris, John, 6–7
Morrison, Jim, 25
Mountain (band), 23t, 192
"Mudstock," 77
Music
    acoustics at Woodstock, 139
    danger of rock music, 79–85
    drug use by musicians, 184–187
    "Heroes of Woodstock" tour, 162
    impact of Woodstock on music events,
        148–150, 156–157
    personal stories and, 184–189
    psychedelic music, 62
    revolving stage, 20, 126
    segmentation of fan base, 149
    sound system at Woodstock, 140
    Woodstock albums, 25, 96, 153
    See also specific musicians
My Lai massacre, 98

N

Nash, Graham, 9, 162, 185
National Advisory Commission on Civil
    Disorders, 150n1
National Guard, 7, 106, 133–134, 181
National Review, 84
National Welfare Rights Organization, 114
New Jersey, 76
New Left Notes (Students for a Democratic
    Society), 66

New Mexico, 17

New York City Police Department, 17, 19

New York State Thruway, 19, 51, 133, 169, 191, 195

New York Times, 5, 7–8, 75, 122, 126–127, 134, 163

Newseum, 8

Newsweek, 195

Nine Inch Nails, 174

Nixon, Richard, 25, 37, 39, 105, 113

NRA (National Rifle Association), 113

Nudity, 58, *61,* 64–65, 105

O

Obama, Barack, 94, 101, 119, 163

Office of Economic Opportunity, 113

P

Pakistan, 119

Paul Butterfield Blues Band, 28t, 192

Paulson, Kenneth A., 8

"Peace Service Corps," 17

Pearl Harbor, 124

Pearl Jam, 27

Pepsi-Cola, 164, 172, 174–175

Peraza, Armando, 142

Personal stories
  comparison of original Woodstock with sequels, 199–203
  David Crosby, 184–189
  French visitor, 190–193
  photographer, 194–198
  teenager at Woodstock, 177–183

Peyote, 62

Pike, Bishop, 43

Pink Floyd, 62

Pink Panthers, 33

Pinkerton, 32

Plant, Robert, 39

Plenk, Bruce, 114, 119

Pomerantz, Rocky, 32

Pomeroy, Wes, 17, 30–44

Poster, *14,* 24, 107, 140, 162–163

Potter, Sean, 72–77

Poverty programs, 111–112

Psilocybin, 62

Psychedelic music, 62, 142

Q

Quicksilver Messenger Service, 62

Quill, 23t

R

Rashomon (Kurosawa), 5

Rathke, Wade, 114, *115,* 119

Reagan, Ronald, 154

"Reagan Democrats," 154

Red Cross, 23, 92

Redding, Otis, 143

Relix (magazine), 157

Republican National Convention of 1964, 36

Republican National Convention of 1968, 37

Reynolds, Susan, 177–183

Rhino Records, 162

Road to Woodstock (Lang), 45–57, 97, 161

Roberts, John
  location of Woodstock festival and, 47, 54–55
  money loss on Woodstock, 91
  security and, 38–39, 43–44

venture capitalist, 143–144
wife, 157
Woodstock Ventures and, 7, 16
Roberts, Rona, 157
Rock and Roll Hall of Fame, 140, 163, 184
Rockefeller, Nelson, 7, 133–134
Rodrick, Stephen, 171–175
Rolie, Gregg, 142
Rolling Stone (magazine), 9, 99, 124, 160
Rolling Stones Altamont concert, 24–25, 98, 135, 137n1, 193, 198
Romney, Hugh (Wavy Gravy), 7, 64, 104–106, 116
Rosenman, Joel
   festival security and, 39
   location of Woodstock festival and, 47, 54
   venture capitalist, 143–144
   Woodstock Ventures and, 7, 16, 158

S

Sander, Ellen, 147
Sanitation
   repair, 63
   problems, 4, 59
   shortages, 147
   toilet paper, 106
   toilets, 22, 47, 140, 180
Santana, Carlos, 23t, 25, 96, 99, 142, *145*, 192
Schwerdtfeger, Patrick, 160
Sebastian, John, 16, 18t, 192
Security
   Christians for Social Action and, 31, 42
   Hoffman and, 89, 104, 135
   Hog Farm Commune of Santa Fe, 89, 104, 135
   Pomeroy and, 17, 30–44
   search for security chief, 31–32
   unarmed security personnel, 38
   Woodstock and, 32–33
Seva foundation, 116
Sha Na Na, 28
Shankar, Ravi, 18
Short Line Bus Company, 89
Shriver, Jerry, 151–158
Sinclair, John, 33–34, 44n2
Sirius XM, 153, 157
Sit-ins, 141, 181
Skolnick, Arnold, 24, 107
Slick, Grace, 189, 192
Slogans, 27, 164, 170, 172, 181
Sobran, Joseph, 102–110
Solar energy, 119
Solomon, Michael, 163
Sommer, Bert, 18t
Sony, 154
Spin (magazine), 165
Stallings, Mark, 154
Stallings, Penny, 50
Stills, Stephen, 188, *See also* Crosby, Stills and Nash
Stone, Sly, 23t, 188
Stonewall riots, 141
Strawberry Alarm Clock, 62
Students for a Democratic Society, 66
Summer of love (1967), 143, 169
Sweetwater, 18t

T

Tactical Execution, 160
Taking Woodstock (movie), 135, 154, 161
Tamarkin, Jeff, 165
Tate, Sharon, 98, 195

Ten Years After, 16, 28t

Tiber, Elliot, 50, 51

Time (magazine), 108, 125, 127, 139

Toledo, Gabe, 156

Townshend, Pete, 27, 96, 105

Traffic problems
  attendees, 59–60, 125, 178
  Frankly Dankly bus and, 117
  media reports, 195
  musicians and, 19–20
  New York State Thruway jam, 19, 51, 133, 169, 191, 195
  predictions, 34
  public transportation and, 89–90

U

University of Pittsburgh, 84

US Army, 106

US Postal Service, 140

US Supreme Court, 98

USA Today, 8, 154

Uzzle, Burk, 194–198, *196*

V

Vietnam War
  activist movement and, 114, 137, 141, *179*, 181–182
  counterculture movement and, 33
  family divisions, 177, 178
  Max Yasgur and, 6
  troop withdrawal, 74
  veterans, 196
  Woodstock and, 156, 160

Village Voice, 165

Violence, 24–25, 33

VISTA (Volunteers in Service to America), 113

Volkswagen, 163

W

Wadleigh, Michael, 96, 98–101, 135, 148

Wall Street Journal, 79–85, 101

Wallkillers, 46–48, 57n1

War on Poverty, 111

Warner Brothers, 96, 161

Washington Post, 125

Water shortages, 59, 87, 140, 147, 180

Wavy Gravy (Hugh Romney), 7, 64, 104–106, 116

WDST radio, 202

Weather
  electrical problems and, 99
  garbage problems and, 70
  impact on Woodstock, 4, 7, 8, 70–77, 87
  "Mudstock," 77
  music performances and, 90–91, 105
  photographs, *73, 123*

Wells, Cathy, 196

Wenner, Jann, 124

White Lake, NY, 50–51, 55–56, 59–61, *61*, 63, *81*

White Panther Party, 33, 44n2

The Who, 16, 23t, 96, 103, 192

Wilder, Thornton, 172

Winter, Johnny, 28t, 103

Women's Liberation, 141

Women's Wear Daily, 122

Woodstock: 3 Days of Peace and Music (movie), 162

Woodstock: Music from the Original Soundtrack and More (album), 25

Woodstock: The Summer of Our Lives (Curry), 108

Woodstock Generation, 141, 156

Woodstock (movie), 6, 25, 135, 148

Woodstock Music and Art Fair
   activist movements and, 94–101, 111–121, 136–137
   admission tickets, 72, 91, 122, 125, 148
   advertising and, 116, 159–166
   Aquarian Exposition, 24, 59, 74, 140
   catastrophe predictions, 132–133
   commemoration, *78*, 138–150
   commercialism, 27, 156
   costs, 45, 47–48, 53–55, 68
   criticism, 79–85, 102–110
   death threats and, 133
   deaths, 28–29, 90, 106, 126
   entrance fees, 6–7, 19
   financial losses, 91, 96, 98–99
   leftover debris, 65–66
   legacy, 147–148, 151–158, 161–163
   musicians performing, 18t, 23t, 28t
   mythology, 4–5, 7, 9, 23–25, 28, 106–109, 127–137, 146
   New York City Police Department and, 17, 19
   nudity and, 58, *61*, 64–65
   peacefulness, 86–93, 147
   photographs, *14, 21, 61, 69, 73, 81, 90, 104, 123, 168, 176*
   poster, 107, 162–163
   power failures in New Jersey and, 76
   public reaction, 60, 67–71
   rumors and misinformation, 61–63, 89
   sequels, 26–28, 152, 167–175, 199–203
   stage, 20, 126
   symbols, 160
   water issues, 6
   weather problems, 4, 7–8, 15, 19
   See also Drugs; Food; Hog Farm Commune; Sanitation; Security; Traffic problems; Yasgur, Max; specific performers

Woodstock Nation, 23, 26, 106, 141, 160
Woodstock Nation (Hoffman), 23
Woodstock Two (album), 25
Woodstock Two Festival, 26–28, 203
Woodstock Ventures
   counterculture image, 17–19
   formation, 7, 16
   Hoffman and, 18
   lawsuits, 28
   trademark ownership, 154
Woodstock Wars (Aspen), 22
Woodstock.com, 154

Y

Yasgur Farm
   leftover debris after Woodstock, 65–66
   location of Woodstock festival, 4, 45, 52–57, 59, 74, 169
   personal stories, 200
   preservation of Yasgur Farm, 130–131
   rental cost of Yasgur Farm, 55
   Woodstock commemoration, *78*, 138–150
   Woodstock mythology and, 5
Yasgur Dairy, 54
Yasgur, Max
   bio, 54
   children, 151, 158
   counterculture movement and, 5–6
   photograph, *49*
   presidency and, 5, 23
   speech to Woodstock crowd, 20, 22
Yasgur, Sam, 151, 158
Yippies (Youth International Party), 33, 44n1
Young, Neil, 27
Yuppies, 156

Z

Zimbabwe, 119

Zmigrodski, Maggie, 152

Zmigrodski, Waverly, 152, 155

Zodiac, 24, 107

Zwakman, Schon, 156